W9-AGA-225

Living Without Fear

Living Without Fear

BY WILMA BURTON

GOOD NEWS PUBLISHERS
Westchester, Illinois 60153

Living Without Fear
Copyright © 1981 by Wilma Burton.
First published in 1981 by Good News Publishers,
Westchester, Illinois 60153.

Library of Congress Catalog Card Number 81-65473

ISBN 0-89107-184-9

Printed in the United States of America.

All rights reserved. No part of this publication may be reproduced, stored in a
retrieval system or transmitted in any form by any means, electronic, mechan-
ical, photocopy, recording, or otherwise, without the prior permission of the
publisher, except as provided in USA copyright law.

Bible quotations are taken from *The New Scofield Reference Bible* unless
otherwise noted.

*Dedicated especially to women who are
studying God's Word in order that they may
be better able to cope with living.*

Contents

Foreword

One of the greatest gifts that a parent can give to a child is to raise that child to face life without fear.

Perhaps the chief recommendation I can lend this book is the fact that I am child of the author. My parents sent me fearless into life. There were cautions, of course, there were reserves, but never the maiming, crippling kinds of inordinate prohibitions that keep so many from functioning fully in this frightening age. My mother and father wonderfully preserved for me that capacity of plunging into life, of looking at each day with awe, of cherishing the unusual or the absurd, of laughter.

We were respectful of others' opinions, but not dominated by them. We knew life could be terrible, filled with pain, but that did not hinder our adventures. I am deeply grateful that they did not clip the wings of the flying thing that soars in the child part of me.

Authenticity can always be tested in the home. My mother has valid reason to write this book. Fear is the dark-eyed shadow my mother came to conquer in her own life. I am the happy result of that struggle.

Part of her capacity is due to her deep regard for Scripture. Mother's ability to free me to face life fearlessly is because of roots she has nourished in the rich soil of truth, God's truth. I recommend to you *Living Without Fear*.

For the most personal of reasons, I am confident this book, formed in Bible survey, will help to free many another mother's child.

Karen Burton Mains

Living Without Fear

Chapter 1

Introductory Thoughts on Fear

The thing of which I have
most fear is fear.
> —Michel Eyquem de Montaigne
> *Essays, Book 1,* Chapter 17, 1580

Mankind has long had a problem with fear. Fear has both plagued and preserved the race. As long as Adam and Eve obeyed God, they were free to walk with him in the cool of the evening in the beautiful Garden of Eden. But when sin entered through the temptation and deception of the serpent, fear came with it. Suddenly afraid of God, they hid themselves from him. They now knew as guilty sinners that it is an awful thing to fall into the hands of the living God.

When God confronted them with their disobedience, they blamed someone else for their sin (an evasion typical of man today). Adam blamed "the woman you gave me," and Eve blamed the serpent (Satan). Each had disobeyed God; each received punishment for that disobedience. Sin has its inevitable price, either to be paid by the sinner or to be absorbed in the vicarious suffering of our Lord on the cross.

Children at play sometimes become little Eves and little Adams, each blaming the other for the broken vase or the trampled flower bed. "Mary did it!" "Johnny made me do it." Fear of punishment is often behind such accusations.

KEY NOTE

Fear has an icy flame. It does not burn or sear. It freezes and forms an igloo around its victim. It can be either a sudden or a creeping paralysis. It attacks us all at one time or another, to some degree or other. We are plagued by fear of sickness, embarrassment, failure; fear of being caught for wrongdoing, losing a tennis match, flying in an airplane; fear of storms, our boss, or any one of 1,001 other fears that beset us.

Yet there are seventy-eight "fear nots" in the Bible. These and other verses on "fear" and "the fear of the Lord" add up to more than 365, one for each day in the year. God has the answer for our every fear!

The first reference to fear in the Old Testament is found in Genesis 3:10, when Adam answers God's call of "where art thou?" with "I heard thy voice in the garden, and I was afraid, because I was naked; and I hid myself." Fear first entered the world in the Garden of Eden, and man has been hiding from God ever since.

God's first recorded "fear not" was spoken to Abraham in Genesis 15:1—"Fear not, Abram: I am thy shield, and thy exceedingly great reward." This statement came immediately before God promised Abraham that a son would be born to his wife Sarah in her old age. God made a covenant to bless Abraham through his seed forever; Abraham believed God, and God "counted it to him for righteousness" (Genesis 15:6).

The first "fear not" in the New Testament is found in Matthew 1:20. The angel of the Lord appeared to Joseph in a dream saying, "Fear not to take unto thee Mary, thy wife; for that which is conceived in her is of the Holy Spirit." Joseph had good reason to be fearful of taking Mary as his wife. Marry a woman already with child? But he exercised faith in God, and all fear left him.

When faith enters through the front door, fear slinks out the back way. Faith's peace and calm drive out turbulent quaking and quivering. Faith and fear cannot coexist. Faith with fear is like standing up sitting down or sitting down standing up.

Christianity enables its followers to live without fear. For example, a Christian can have every confidence that although the future may be an unknown to him or her, there are no unknowns to God, who in his omniscience knows the end from the beginning—and all of the in-betweens as well.

The apostles who fled from the trial and crucifixion of Jesus in cowardice and fear, lest they suffer a similar fate, were transformed by the Christ of the Resurrection into men of courage. Many of the apostles even met martyrs' deaths for Christ; their fear had given way to faith. Peter, we are told, asked to be crucified upside down as he felt unworthy to be crucified in the same manner his Lord had been.

In her book *The Hiding Place*, Corrie ten Boom describes the peace God gave her and her sister in the midst of the horrors of the Ravensbruck prison. When her father was asked if he had the grace to die, he said no; he did not yet need it. He compared this to not needing a train ticket until you get to the station. God gives grace to overcome fear as we need it, but rarely before it is needed.

NOTE

In the Gospel of Luke, the first "fear not" of the New Testament (chronologically) was spoken by the angel Gabriel to Zacharias: "Fear not, Zacharias; for thy prayer is heard; and thy wife, Elisabeth, shall bear thee a son, and thou shalt call his name John" (1:13). Zacharias was "stricken in years" and could easily have questioned the angel's promise to him because of his age. But God gave him a sign: he was stricken dumb and did not speak again until John the Baptist was born. God then loosed his tongue, so he could name his newborn son "John."

Perhaps the most important "fear not" of all was Gabriel's to the virgin Mary: "Fear not, Mary; for thou hast found favor with God. And, behold, thou shalt conceive in thy womb, and bring forth a son, and shalt call his name JESUS . . ." (Luke 1:30, 31). The angel Gabriel ended his message to Mary with the words, "For with God nothing shall be impossible" (1:37). As long as we serve a God like that, what have we to fear?

Mary's song of faith, better known as "The Magnificat," expresses her praise to God for choosing her to be the mother of Jesus:

My soul doth magnify the Lord, and my spirit hath rejoiced in God my Savior. For he hath regarded the low estate of his handmaiden; for, behold, from henceforth all generations shall call me blessed. For he that is mighty hath done to me great things; and holy is his name. And his mercy is on them that *fear him* from generation to generation. He hath shown strength with his arm; he hath scattered the proud in the imagination of their hearts. He hath put down the mighty from their seats, and exalted them of low degree. He hath filled the hungry with good things; and the rich he hath sent empty away. He hath helped his servant, Israel, in remembrance of his mercy; as he spoke to our fathers, to Abraham, and to his seed forever. (Luke 1:46-55)

Whenever fear yields to faith, a song follows. Early Christians who were martyred because of their faith did not cower in the catacombs, but marched singing to their deaths in the Roman arena. Paul and Silas didn't quiver in their Roman prison, but sang hymns of praise. The children of Israel, escaping from Pharaoh by night, sang in the wilderness. What a song that must have been, coming from two million men, women, and children rejoicing in their new-found freedom. True, they fell into the sin of murmuring and complaining. But whenever fear departed and faith took command, they sang.

David conquered fear when he killed the lion, the bear, and Goliath. Many were the songs he sang, songs of bravery and the greatness of God. These songs of David have helped all who have read and sung them through the centuries. Through them, fear has been routed and faith has seized the throne.

In the best known of all of his Psalms, the 23rd, he has this to say about fear: "Yea, though I walk through the valley of the shadow of death, *I shall fear no evil;* for thou art with me."

Here we see that the realized presence of the Lord can banish all fear of all evil in the believer's life. What a precious inheritance!

I am not a psychologist formally trained in helping people overcome their fears. I write these chapters from

personal experience. I do presume to be a student of the
Word of God, and it is through a study of the Bible and
what it has to teach us about fear that I write these chapters on *Living Without Fear*. Both my husband and son
majored in psychology, and both concluded that psychology as taught in the universities is strong on diagnoses,
but weak on therapy. The Holy Spirit is a healer of all
man's emotional problems, and his teachings are revealed in the Word of God. Through his leading, the
emotion of fear with all of its phobias can be healed; this
is known as paracaletic psychology, and is explained by
Paul Morris in his book *Love Therapy* (Tyndale House,
1974).

Through the study of the Word, led by the Holy Spirit,
we can be freed from the destructive fears and phobias
that grip our lives and threaten to paralyze us. We can
learn to live without unhealthy fears and to know both
emotional stability and mental health. "For God hath not
given us the spirit of fear, but of power, and of love, and
of a sound mind" (2 Timothy 1:7).

The last "fear" in the Bible (Revelation 21:7, 8) may
have special significance as it is a last word on the subject of fear. "He that overcometh shall inherit all things,
and I will be his God, and he shall be my son. But the
fearful, and unbelieving, and the abominable, and
murderers, and fornicators, and sorcerers, and idolaters,
and all liars, shall have their part in the lake which burneth with fire and brimstone, which is the second death."

Here we see a surprising thing in that the fearful (those
who are full of fear, controlled by fear, or subject to fear)
are included with unbelievers, fornicators, and liars; all
are plunged into the second death. The second death, as

most Bible scholars understand it, is eternal separation from God.

Thus we see that sinful fear is not to be taken lightly. But fear can be dealt a deathblow through a fear of God and faith in Jesus Christ. We will learn more about this as we go along.

In these chapters we shall be exploring three kinds of fear—the all-important *fear of the Lord,* the *protective fears* (such as concern for our loved ones), and the *destructive fears* (such as *fear of death*).

Several years ago, a friend whose teenage son was dying of cancer (and has since died) included with her Christmas card a modern parable which had enabled her to face the death of her son. I have transformed the message into a poem:

Footsteps on the Sands of Time
Last night, I dreamed I walked along a beach
with my Lord. Two sets of tracks our footsteps
made. Then the going grew steep, the path rock-
strewn and one set of footprints disappeared.
"Why did you leave when struggle came," I cried,
"and desperate my need for you?" In the still
of the night, my Lord so gently replied
in a voice of love: "I would not forsake
you, my child—remember, for you I died—
the one set of prints is when I carried you!"

Chapter 2

The Fear of the Lord:
Cradle of Wisdom

And lips say "God be pitiful,"
Who ne'er said, "God be praised."
— Elizabeth Barrett Browning,
"The Cry of the Human"

Not all fear is evil, nor are all fears harmful. In fact, one specific "fear" is essential to meaningful, happy living. It is the fear of God.

This fear is described by Webster as "awe, profound reverence, especially for the Supreme Being." Reverence is further explained as "veneration; honor; respect; act of obeisance; a title given to clergy (with his, your); v.t. to regard with reverence."

In Isaiah 9:6 *(The Living Bible)* we read some of the names given to Christ: "These will be his royal titles: 'Wonderful,' 'Counselor,' 'The Mighty God,' 'The Everlasting Father,' 'The Prince of Peace.' " We thrill to hear these words sung in the "Hallelujah Chorus" (from Handel's *Messiah*). Perhaps we have pictured God too often as "sweet little Jesus boy" to our children and have neglected to stress the fact that he is the mighty Maker of the universe. His hands control the stars and seas, support the heavens, undergird the earth and all the thousands of galaxies in outer space that are dependent upon his laws. He is indeed a great God before whom we can but bow in reverence.

Some years ago, the Greater Europe Mission published a list of the more than 200 names for our Lord that are found in the Bible. I list them here, for a study of God's names can help us have a greater reverence for him.

> ". . .and a book of remembrance was
> written . . . for them that . . .
> thought upon his name. . ."

(Malachi 3:16)

Jesus • the Young Child • Thy Holy Child • the Nazarene • Jesus of Nazareth • Lord • Lord Jesus • the Lord from Heaven • the Lord of Glory • the Lord our Righteousness • the Lord of the Holy Prophets • Lord and Saviour • my Lord and my God • the Holy One of God.

Jesus Christ • Christ Jesus • Lord and Christ • the Lord's Christ • the Christ of God • Lord Jesus Christ • Lord of Sabaoth • Lord of Hosts • Lord of the Sabbath • Lord of Heaven and Earth • Jesus Christ our Lord • Our Lord and Saviour Jesus Christ • the Saviour of the World.

Jesus Christ the Righteous • Saviour • Emmanuel • Teacher • Rabboni • Master • Governor • Law Giver • Forerunner • Redeemer • Messiah • Shiloh • Deliverer • Mediator • Intercessor • Messiah and Prince • a Prince and a Saviour • Mighty to Save.

Surety of a Better Testament • the Just One • the Holy One • the Holy and the Just • the Holy and Righteous One • the Holy One of God • the Faithful and True Witness • a Witness to the

People • a Leader and Commander of the People • the Consolation of Israel • the Lion of the Tribe of Judah.

First Fruits • the First Begotten • the Elect of God • a Branch of Righteousness • the Second Adam • the Last Adam • King of Zion • King of the Jews • the King of Israel • the King of Saints • the Prince of the Kings of the Earth • the King Eternal • Immortal • Invisible • God Manifest in the Flesh.

The Righteous Judge • the Judge of Israel • the Judge of all the Earth • the Desire of all the Nations • the Ensign of the People • the Captain of the Lord's Host • a Banner Upon the High Mountain.

Messenger of the Covenant • a Minister of the Sanctuary • the Author and Finisher of our Faith • Our Advocate • Our Advocate with the Father • Our Peace • Our Ransom • Our Passover • Our Great High Priest • a High Priest forever after the order of Melchisedec • King of Righteousness • King of Salem • King of Peace.

The Man Christ Jesus • a Man Approved of God • Our Elder Brother • the First Born among many Brethren • a Friend that sticketh closer than a brother • the Master • Your Master • Your Lord and Master • Good Master.

Horn of Salvation • the Captain of our Salvation • the Brightness of the Father's Glory • the Glory as of the Only Begotten • the Image of the Invisible God • the Express Image of His Person • the Fullness of the Godhead Bodily • the Bridegroom • the Beginning of the Creation of God.

The Way • the Truth • the Life • the Tree of Life • the Light of Life • the Word of Life • the Bread of Life • the Prince of Life • Life Eternal • the Water of Life • the Living Water • the Living Bread • the Bread which came down from Heaven • the True Bread from Heaven • the Hidden Manna.

The Door • the Door of the Sheep • the Chief Shepherd • the Good Shepherd • that Great Shepherd of the Sheep • the Shepherd and Bishop of your souls • a Lamb without Spot or Blemish • a Lamb Slain before the Foundation of the World.

The Vine • the True Vine • the Root of Jesse • the Root and Offspring of David • Prophet of Nazareth • a Prophet Mighty in

Word and Deed • the Prophet of the Highest.

The Day Star • the Day Spring from on High • Heir of All Things • a Tried Stone • a Living Stone • an Elect Stone • a Sure Foundation • a stone • chosen of God and Precious • that Rock • that Spiritual Rock • the Rock of Ages • Faithful and True Witness • the Apostle and High Priest of our Profession • I AM.

Man of Sorrows • a Friend of Sinners • the Gift of God • the Unspeakable Gift • God Blessed Forever • Light of the World • a quickening Spirit • the First Fruits of them that sleep • the First Begotten of the Dead • the Resurrection and the Life.

The Head of the Corner • the Head of the Church • the Head of every Man • the True Light which lighteth every man which cometh into the world.

Rose of Sharon • the Lily of the Valley • the One Altogether Lovely • the Fairest Among Ten Thousand • the Bright and Morning Star.

The Power of God • the Wisdom of God • the Gift of God • the Word of God • the Image of God • the Lamb of God which taketh away the sin of the world • God's Elect.

The First and the Last • the Beginning and the End • Alpha and Omega • Ancient of Days • King of Kings and Lord of Lords • Blessed and Only Potentate • God With Us • God Our Saviour • the Only Wise God Our Saviour • the Lord Which Is • Which Was • Which Is to Come • Almighty.

The Son of Mary • the Son of Man • the Son of David • the Son of Abraham • the Son of the Blessed • the Son of Righteousness • the Son of the Highest • My Son • the Son of God • the Son of the Living God • God's Dear Son • the Son of His Love • the Only Begotten Son of God • this is My Beloved Son in Whom I am Well Pleased.

> "For unto us a child is born and unto
> us a son is given and the government
> shall be upon his shoulders and his
> name shall be called Wonderful,
> Counsellor, the Mighty God, the Ever-
> lasting Father, the Prince of Peace!"

—Isaiah 9:6

The more than two hundred names of our Lord were compiled by Clinton N. Howard after he was challenged by a Moslem nobleman saying his rosary which included ninety-nine names for Allah. Mr. Howard published these names in 1925 under the title, "Pearls of Paradise," at the request of William Jennings Bryan.

Cruden's Concordance tells us that "The fear of God means that reverence for God which leads to obedience because of one's realization of his power, as well as of his love to man." Standing in awe before God's unlimited power and his unconditional love—this is reverence.

The Book of Job, thought to be the oldest book in the Bible, is the first of the Wisdom Books in the Old Testament canon, the others being Proverbs and Ecclesiastes. Wisdom literature, of which the Epistle of James in the New Testament is an example, deals with the broad realm of human experience, and is set forth in short, pithy sayings (proverbs), essays, monologues, and (as in Job) drama.

It is singular that in this drama, whose theme is the problem of suffering, we find the fear of God mentioned in the very first verse of the very first chapter. "There was a man in the land of Uz, whose name was Job; and that man was perfect and upright, and one that *feared God*, and shunned evil."

Job was a patriarch with seven sons and three daughters, 7,000 sheep, 3,000 camels, 500 yoke of oxen, and 500 female donkeys, and a very great household; he was the greatest of all the men of the east. This great man feared God, even bringing burnt offerings for his sons and daughters, saying, "It may be that my sons have sinned, and cursed God in their hearts."

Now there was a day when the sons of God came to present themselves before the Lord, and Satan came also among them. And the Lord said unto Satan, From where comest thou? Then Satan answered the Lord, and said, From going to and fro in the earth, and from walking up and down in it. And the Lord said unto Satan, Hast thou considered my servant, Job, that there is none like him in the earth, a perfect and an upright man, one who *feareth God*, and shunneth evil? Then Satan answered the Lord, Doth Job *fear God* for nothing? Hast thou not made an hedge about him, and about his house, and about all that he hath on every side? Thou hast blessed the work of his hands, and his substance is increased in the land. But put forth thine hand now, and touch all that he hath, and he will curse thee to thy face. (Job 1:6-11)

We see Satan coming before the Lord a second time, and God says to him,

From where comest thou? And Satan answered the Lord, and said, From going to and fro in the earth, and from walking up and down in it. And the Lord said unto Satan, Hast thou considered my servant, Job, that there is none like him in the earth, a perfect and an upright man, one that *feareth God*, and shunneth evil? And still he holdeth fast his integrity, although thou movedst me against him, to destroy him without cause. (Job 2:2, 3)

In the second testing which God permitted, we see Job covered with boils from the sole of his foot to the crown of his head. His wife tells him to "Curse God, and die," but Job continues to trust in God. "What?" he asks, "shall we receive only pleasant things from the hand of God and never anything unpleasant?" (Job 2:10, TLB).

Job's fear of the Lord was important enough to be described in the first book of the Scriptures to be written. God permitted him to be severely tested by Satan and that testing was recorded by an unknown writer, moved of course by the Holy Spirit, for future consideration of all the generations to be born after Job's lifetime. The fear of the Lord must, therefore, be of prime importance in the life of every believer (and nonbeliever) today.

Job quotes God as saying, "And unto man he said, Behold, the fear of the Lord, that is wisdom; and to depart from evil is understanding" (28:28).

Some of the Old Testament saints so feared the Lord that they came through the severest of tests praising God. For example, in Exodus 1:17 we read, "But the midwives feared God, and did not as the king of Egypt commanded them, but saved the male children alive." Their fear of the Lord caused the midwives to obey God rather than the wicked law of Pharaoh.

In every culture, man tends to put his highest and noblest thoughts into poetry. It was so in Bible times. We find many references to the fear of the Lord in the poetic books of the Old Testament: Job, Psalms, Proverbs, Song of Solomon, Ecclesiastes. For example:

The fear of the Lord prolongeth days. (Proverbs 10:27)

Better is little with the fear of the Lord, than great treasure and trouble therewith. (Proverbs 15:16)

The fear of the Lord tendeth to life, and he who hath it shall abide satisfied; he shall not be visited with evil. (Proverbs 19:23)

The fear of the Lord was a favorite subject of the early poets whether they were dealing in Job with the problem of pain, or teaching in Psalms the way to pray, or in Proverbs the behavior of the believer, or in Ecclesiastes the folly of forgetting God, or in the Song of Solomon the art of adoration. It is evident in the Hebrews' hymns, dirges, dramas, elegies, epics, idylls, lyrics, and odes.

Solomon, known for his wisdom, wrote in Proverbs 1:7, "The fear of the Lord is the beginning of knowledge, but fools despise wisdom and instruction." A footnote in *The New Scofield Reference Bible* explains that "fool" in Scripture does not denote "a mentally deficient person but rather one who is arrogant and self-sufficient, one who orders his life as if there were no God." The rich man referred to in Luke 12:16-21 was not mentally inferior, but he was a "fool" because he supposed that his soul could live on the things in his barn, giving no thought to his eternal well-being.

Again in Proverbs, Solomon admonishes:

The fear of the Lord is to hate evil; pride, and arrogance, and the evil way, and the perverse mouth, do I hate. (8:13)

The fear of the Lord is the beginning of wisdom, and the knowledge of the Holy One is understanding. (9:10)

In the fear of the Lord is strong confidence, and his children shall have a place of refuge. (14:26)

The fear of the Lord is a fountain of life, to depart from the snares of death. (14:27)

The fear of the Lord is the instruction of wisdom; and before honor is humility. (15:33)

Favor is deceitful, and beauty is vain, but a woman who feareth the Lord, she shall be praised. (31:30)

Fearing God is emphasized throughout the Old Testament. For example:

In Genesis 22:12 we hear the Lord speaking to Abraham after the patriarch's severe testing and his placing his beloved son, Isaac, on the altar of sacrifice (a foreshadowing of the sacrifice of Christ and his obedience to death): "For now I know that thou fearest God, seeing thou hast not withheld thy son, thine only son from me."

Deuteronomy records the Lord's saying to Moses. "Oh, that there were such an heart in them, that they would fear me, and keep all my commandments always, that it might be well with them and with their children forever!" (Deuteronomy 5:29).

In that same book we read:

And now, Israel, what doth the Lord thy God require of thee, but to fear the Lord thy God, to walk in all his ways, and to love him, and to serve the Lord thy God with all thy heart and with all thy soul. (10:12)

Joshua commanded the people of Israel:

Now, therefore, fear the Lord, and serve him in sincerity and in truth; and put away the gods which your fathers served on the other side of the river, and in Egypt, and serve ye the Lord. (Joshua 24:14)

Isaiah exhorted the believing remnant:

Sanctify the Lord of hosts himself, and let him be your fear, and let him be your dread. (8:13)

Jeremiah added:

And I will give them one heart, and one way, that they may fear me forever, for the good of them, and of their children after them. And I will make an everlasting covenant with them, that I will not turn away from doing them good, but I will put my fear in their hearts, that they shall not depart from me. (32:39, 40).

Another reference to the faithful remnant occurs in Malachi 3:16—

Then they that feared the Lord spoke often one to another;
and the Lord hearkened, and heard it, and a book of remembrance was written before him for them that feared the Lord,
and that thought upon his name.

The New Testament continues to stress the importance
of fearing the Lord.

Let us have grace, by which we may serve God acceptably
with reverence and godly fear; for our God is a consuming fire.
(Hebrews 12:28, 29)

But sanctify the Lord God in your hearts, and be ready
always to give an answer to every man that asketh you a reason
of the hope that is in you, with meekness and fear. (1 Peter
3:15)

To fear the Lord is to reverence him. And to reverence
him is to love good and to hate evil (in other words, to
love what God loves and to hate what he hates).

So we see that fearing God is a healthy, in fact essential thing to do if we are to have a joyful, God-pleasing
life.

On the other hand, "the fearful . . . shall have their
part in the lake which burneth with fire and brimstone"
(Revelation 21:8). When we do not fear God, reverenc-
ing and obeying him, we are victims of the many fears
that abound in this world. As someone has commented,
"He who fears God need fear nothing else, and he who
fears not God needs to fear everything else." George
MacDonald adds, "Fear is faithlessness." A lack of faith
opens up a world of fear with the ultimate result being
separation from God. What could be more important than
to fear God in our hearts and to obey him as our omnipo-
tent Ruler and King of kings?

FOOD FOR THOUGHT
1. *Have you received Christ as your personal Savior?*
2. *List some salvation verses that give you assurance.*
3. *Is being obedient to God more important to you than pleasing men?*
4. *Do you find joy in obeying God, in preferring his will over your own?*

Chapter 3
The Holy War Between Fears

You call for faith:
I show you doubt, to prove that faith exists.
The more of doubt, the stronger faith, I say
If faith o'ercomes doubt.
> —Robert Browning,
> "Bishop Blougram's Apology"

Webster defines what we shall term *healthy fear* as a "state of anxious concern, solicitude." It differs from *unhealthy fear*, in that it demands action, not just mental distress. For example, a mother may have a son who catches colds easily. On a wintry day, her fear for the child demands action. She either brings him inside out of the wind and cold, or she takes him a warm sweater with a hood and sees that he puts it on. Her fear is healthy; it stems from a normal concern.

Unhealthy fear is described by Webster as "painful emotion marked by alarm, dread, disquiet, also an instance of this feeling; ground for occasion of alarm, danger. Fear, dread, fright, alarm, dismay, consternation, panic, apprehension, anxiety.'' Unhealthy fear produces worry, which is an underlying cause of hypertension, heart attacks, strokes, and related diseases of the body. It inhibits, immobilizes, paralyzes.

The fear of the Lord is a healthy fear (fear here not meaning, of course, dread but reverence). God is loving and full of mercy, but he is also the Righteous Judge who hates sin and evil. When a man dares to take lightly Christ's sacrifice on the cross, he is the victim of rank folly. God will not extend his mercy forever to those who refuse to heed his teachings. There is a point of no return on the downward path of the sinner. Fearing God and his judgment is certainly a healthy fear. Awe and profound reverence for the Supreme Being does not involve a buddy-buddy relationship with the Creator, but rather the respectful relationship a child should have with his father.

Healthy fear never paralyzes or cripples. In fact, it carries with it the ability to act, to exercise courage.

Our son, not yet two, slipped out the door into the cool darkness of a winter night, dressed only in an undershirt, diaper, shoes, and socks. A driver who saw him running precariously on the snowy walk picked up the shivering child and brought him to our door. Healthy fear is protective. It demands action, sometimes immediate action. It is a special gift from God. Henry Ward Beecher composed these beautiful words:

God planted fear in the soul as truly as he planted hope or courage. It is a kind of bell or gong which rings the mind into quick life and avoidance on the approach of danger. It is the soul's signal for rallying.

Fear of drowning may make an individual wear a life jacket. A healthy fear of an accident may cause the driver to wear his seat belt and to insist that his passengers fasten theirs as well.

Healthy fear is seldom, if ever, passive. It is related to love and kindness, and the preservation of life. But unguarded, it can easily become an unhealthy fear, a destructive preoccupation.

A fear of eating wild mushrooms is a healthy fear. Distinguishing a good mushroom from a poisonous one is a job for an expert in the field of botany, and a mistake can lead to illness and even hospitalization—or worse, death. But this could become an unhealthy fear should an individual decide *never* to eat any mushrooms in any shape or form, whether wild or cultivated.

Everyone has some healthy fears, and it is well to keep such cautions alive—but controlled. Are you afraid to invest your money in wildcat money-making schemes? Or to let your toddler play unguarded near a busy street? Or to let your preteenager drive the car without a driver's license or permit? Or to drive your car as fast as you can through a school zone? Or to let your car insurance lapse? Or to let your children fail to keep dental appointments? Or to let your aged mother walk unaided up ice-coated steps? When burglars are on the increase in your area, are you afraid to leave your house unlocked?

Do you fear the consequence of not having your children properly immunized against diseases such as measles, diphtheria, polio, tetanus? Do you fear lying on the beach under a torpid sun too long lest your tan turn into a red peeling blister, and maybe into sun cancer?

In extremes of cold, are you afraid that without proper

clothing you may suffer from exposure and end up with pneumonia? Are you afraid to start out on a long trip with badly worn tires? Or, if you are a student, are you afraid to take an important exam without studying or at least reviewing for it? These are all healthy fears and are not to be avoided, but rather to be used for your own good and the welfare of others.

Of course, this is all somewhat relative too. For the person past middle age, who is not in good physical condition, a fear of jogging may be a healthy fear. Jogging can preface a heart attack in an older person not accustomed to exercise. But for the runner, such as my son, jogging is a healthy exercise and keeps him in good physical condition. However, since he ran twenty-six miles in the Drake Marathon, he has been having trouble with his knees. A valid fear of continued knee trouble has caused him to give up his jogging for a while and to swim several times a week for a less strenuous form of exercise. To recognize the difference between healthy fear and unhealthy fear demands wisdom.

Unhealthy fears, if not properly checked, turn into phobias. Many thousands of dollars are paid each year by patients to psychiatrists in an endeavor to learn to overcome and cope with fear.

A healthy fear of fire can turn into pyrophobia. A normal fear of fire will act as a caution to keep matches out of the reach of small children, to see that children's clothing is not made of inflammable materials, etc. A person suffering from an unhealthy fear of fire, on the other hand, may refuse to have candles or even matches in his house, or to let anyone light the fireplace, or refuse to use a gas dryer or cooking stove, or to permit the burning of leaves even in a wire burner made for that purpose. Unchecked by wisdom and common sense, fear may develop many forms of neurosis.

A fear of water may start out as a healthy fear and cause one to use caution in boating or swimming. But when it is carried to the point where the individual suffers from an unhealthy fear of water, the person may refuse any and all forms of boat travel, even safe ocean liners, or even to wade in a pool although that pool may be supervised by a lifeguard. In extreme instances of aquaphobia, the victim actually may be afraid of bathing in a bathtub. This unhealthy fear may be the result of a near-drowning experience as a child, or perhaps losing a loved one by drowning.

Many a harmful fear has its roots in childhood. Perhaps a small child is shut in a closet for punishment by an unwise parent, sibling, or baby sitter. From what was to him a terror experience, the child develops claustrophobia that remains with him into his adult years. He cannot ride on elevators or buses, or be in other small rooms, or even ride in a car full of people without mental agony.

In some cases, psychiatrists are able to help—for a fee, of course! But too often the psychiatrist can diagnose, but cannot come up with a cure. Especially is this true if he has no biblical background.

Faith in God as "a rewarder of them that diligently seek him" routs fear in the believer. Unhealthy fear, worry, and anxiety have no place in the Christian's life. In these pages we are going to look closely at God's Word, find his teachings (he is the greatest psychiatrist of all), and seek to overcome through his help any and all unhealthy fears in our lives. The promise in Romans 8:28 ("And we know that all things work together for good to them that love God, to them who are the called according to his purpose") has been and is a great force in helping the believer cope with fear in his or her life. Notice that I have said "believer," for while this verse is sometimes quoted by unbelievers and even by some who are admittedly agnostics, it does not apply to their lives. It is privileged to "them that love God."

Unhealthy fear is actually damaging to the body. Acting like a boa constrictor, it constricts the blood vessels. It is the cause of many heart attacks. Persons who are full of such fears are often the victims of myocardia infarct or coronary occlusion—a closing of the arteries that lead to the heart, and thus restricting the blood flow to and from the heart.

Of course, God can use *anything* (remember Romans 8:28) for our ultimate good. Even unhealthy fears can draw us closer to God in our relationship with him as Creator, Father, Physician. But basically we either learn to walk in faith and so control the unholy fears that plague our lives, or they will in time control us and defeat us spiritually, emotionally, and physically. As others have said:

Our greatest enemies are not wild beasts or deadly germs but fears that paralyze thought, poison the mind, and destroy character. Our only protection against fear is faith. (Phyllis Goslin Lynip, in *Great Ideas of the Bible*)

Since fear is unreasonable, never try to reason with it. So-called "positive thinking" is no weapon against fear. Only positive faith can rout the black menace of fear and give life a radiance. (Marion Hilliard, in *Digest of World Reading*)

A perfect faith would lift us absolutely above fear. (George MacDonald)

Unhealthy fear and faith are antithetical. They cannot coexist. As the inscription over the mantel in the Hind's Head Hotel in England says, "Fear knocked at the door. Faith answered. No one was there." No fear is strong enough to resist genuine Christian faith.

Whenever a healthy fear grows out of control, it becomes a spiritual cancer, resulting in undue worry and stress. In addition to causing physical illnesses such as high blood pressure, ulcers, colitis and other diseases of the digestive tract and circulation, heart trouble, strokes, it can also produce mental illnesses such as deep depression and serious paranoid conditions so common in our world. Unhealthy fears can also cause social ostracism, family dissension, and divorce.

But there is a cure: "Be anxious for nothing, but in everything, by prayer and supplication with thanksgiving, let your requests be made known unto God" (Philippians 4:6). This is not a mere suggestion to follow or not follow, depending on our own feelings at the moment. It is a command from God, and we dare not ignore it.

Verse 7 continues, "And the peace of God, which passeth all understanding, shall keep your hearts and minds through Christ Jesus." Through Christ, and only through Christ, we can have peace, total freedom from fear.

Drop thy still dews of quietness till all our striving cease;
Take from our souls the strain and stress,
And let our ordered lives confess
The beauty of thy peace.
                          —John Greenleaf Whittier

Verse 8 adds, "Finally, brethren, whatever things are true, whatever things are honest, whatever things are just, whatever things are pure, whatever things are lovely, whatever things are of good report; if there be any virtue, if there be any praise, think on these things." If we fill our thoughts with these things, there will be no room for fear.

Verse 9 tells us that if we follow the instructions of the previous verses, "the God of peace shall be with you."

Unholy fear must flee when we practice the presence of the God of peace and fill our minds with good thoughts.

What shall separate us from the love of Christ? Shall tribulation, or distress, or persecution, or famine, or nakedness, or peril, or sword? As it is written, For thy sake we are killed all the day long; we are accounted as sheep for the slaughter. Nay, in all these things we are more than conquerors through him that loved us. For I am persuaded that neither death, nor life, nor angels, nor principalities, nor powers, nor things present, nor things to come, nor height, nor depth, nor any other creature, shall be able to separate us from the love of God, which is in Christ Jesus, our Lord. (Romans 8:35-39)

A friend recently said to me, "I seem to be able to stand the elephant testings when they come, but it is the little everyday mouse nibblings that throw me." Are you a victim of these little nibblings, little anxieties, little fears that beg for the food of your attention so they can grow into the Gargantuans of unhealthy fears? As the song says, "Give them all to Jesus!" "Casting all your care upon him; for he careth for you" (1 Peter 5:7).

When we remain in the smile of God's grace, both our healthy fears and unholy fears are under his control. Walking in the fear of the Lord is a joyful walk, and the path is adorned with bright flowers of blessing.

FOOD FOR THOUGHT
1. *List the healthy fears in your life.*
2. *List the unhealthy fears that trouble you now or from time to time.*
3. *Memorize 2 Timothy 1:7.*

Chapter 4

Fear of the Dragons of Darkness

Life is a dream in the night,
a fear among fears,
A naked runner lost
in a storm of spears.
>   —Arthur Symons,
>   "Memory"

It is not uncommon for children to develop phobias in early childhood that they carry with them all their lives. For many years I suffered from a "mouse phobia." In the first month of our marriage, my husband was shocked to find me screaming from the top of the kitchen table where I had leaped at the sight of an innocent field mouse that had come into our farm kitchen to escape the cold.

This phobia had started when I was three. I had seen a mouse scurry behind my mother's sewing machine, and thought I would chase it out with a yardstick. This I managed to do, but the little creature ran along my bare arm and frightened me until my screams brought both parents running. The fright did not end there, for I suffered from nightmares many months afterwards.

Fortunately, our family home has been mouse-proof, but the farmhouse that became my concern after my husband's illness was quite a different story. The field mice loved it! Each fall they held their family reunions in every room. Through prayer, I learned to set traps and catch them. But I must admit to an extravagance of sometimes throwing out mouse, trap and all. I realize it was a ridiculous fear, but it was very real to me for many years. And even now, I enjoy the comfort of knowing there are no mice in the house. I tell this story to help you examine your own leftover childish fears in the light of your more mature years.

Fear of the dark is a childhood fear that often carries over into adulthood too. I know grown persons who prefer to keep a light burning—if not in their rooms, in a nearby hall or bathroom (for the sake of their children, of course).

I well remember my own fear of the dark when I was a small child. It seemed every imaginable monster came out of the walls as soon as the light was put out. ("Put out" is accurate, for we had gas lights in our house that had to be extinguished and lit again with a match. Once they were out, it was not as simple as flicking a light switch to appease a child who was afraid of the dark.)

My brother was two years younger than I, but he delighted in trying to frighten me at night when the lights were out. Often his wicked imaginings ricocheted on him, and he was as afraid of his imagined dragons and hobgoblins as I was. How we would quake under our covers and call for a drink of water (a ruse to get a parent back into our room for protection).

Why are we so afraid of the dark? Perhaps we fear the unknown, the mysterious, the unseeable. But most of all, it is because we exercise so little genuine faith in God. It is God who drives out our darkness. "God, who commanded the light to shine out of darkness, hath shone in our hearts, to give the light of the knowledge of the glory of God in the face of Jesus Christ" (2 Corinthians 4:6).

The fear of darkness when carried to an extreme can become unhealthy, but when used in wisdom it can be beneficial. We can learn from flowers who see the light and climb each day toward the sun. It is wise when we must be out at night to seek to stay within lighted areas; studies show that crime decreases when cities install good lighting systems. Criminal minds love the cover of darkness in which to work evil, because they have refused the one true Light who came into the world, Jesus Christ. "And this is the condemnation, that light is come into the world, and men loved darkness rather than light, because their deeds were evil" (John 3:19). But even though such evil is done in it, must we fear darkness?

One of my grandchildren, a highly imaginative child, developed a strong fear of the dark. He did not like to go to bed alone, but would stay up until an older brother could accompany him. His sleep was broken by nightmares, with various monsters of his imagination filling his room and mind. My daughter consistently taught him Scriptures that had to do with fear. Imagine our delight when, on a dare from his older brother, he spent the night alone in the unoccupied upstairs of our farmhouse without a light burning. The little frightened boy of four and five had grown into a brave lad of eight. If he was afraid during the night. Joel did not let his older brother know it. I don't doubt but that he spent his awake moments repeating the Bible verses on fear his mother had taught him.

Another strong factor in Joel's lack of fear is that he had given his heart to the Lord Jesus several months before and had actually become a new creature in Christ (see 2 Corinthians 5:17). Christian faith drives out fear. As Helen Keller put it, "A simple, childlike faith in a Divine Friend solves all the problems that come to us by land or sea."

One evening not long ago, I found it necessary, through a series of unusual circumstances, to approach my dark house with the back door unlocked. Knowing there had been a number of break-ins in our neighborhood in the past months, I found myself repeating Psalm 23 as I entered.

That evening, a friend picked me up and remarked as I got into her car, "Is your mother with you? I thought I saw two people through your living room window."

Later, when I returned from the concert we had attended, I remembered her remark and realized there could have been someone else in my house; I had been gone for several hours with the house unlocked. I turned the lights on as I entered the kitchen and stood perfectly quiet to see if there were any unusual sounds in my house (nothing but the rather loud beating of my heart). I walked across the kitchen carpeting and checked the basement door, which was unlocked. I keep this locked, because if anyone were to break into my home it would probably be through a basement window. Should I call the police? The question did enter my mind, but I brushed it aside.

I went to bed with no fear in my heart, read several Psalms, and knew that I was safe in God's keeping. Without the Holy Spirit, this experience could have been one of fear and trauma. God is greater than our fear. Fear never comes from him, but rather from the powers of darkness that no longer have dominion over us. I have lived alone in my big old family home for several years now and can attest to the fact that unhealthy fear is not a part of my life. Rather, I am aware of the presence of the Holy Spirit both day and night—and he has promised *never to leave me, never to leave me alone.*

Luke 21:26 pictures "men's hearts failing them for fear" in the end times. Many men are dying of fear in our lifetime. During the crash of '29, many committed suicide because they were afraid to live without their stock holdings. In her autobiography, Helen Steiner Rice tells that her husband of two years committed suicide when the stock market failed. Fear or faith—that's our choice.

Recently I traveled with my son-in-law through Kentucky. He told me of his visit as a child of ten to Mammoth Cave. His guide impressed his young mind with a story (whether truth or fiction, he did not know) about early explorers in the cave whose bodies were later found bleached white, both hair and skin. This was thought to be caused by the fright they experienced when their lamps burned out and they found themselves stranded in the darkest dark the world knows, in the middle of the earth, with not a pinprick of light present.

In Matthew 25:30 we read, "And cast the unprofitable servant into outer darkness; there shall be weeping and gnashing of teeth." The believer shall never know this outer darkness, for "Unto the upright there ariseth light in the darkness; he is gracious, and full of compassion, and righteous" (Psalm 112:4). This light comes to us through Jesus Christ, "the light of the world." "He that followeth me shall not walk in darkness, but shall have the light of life," Jesus promises in John 8:12.

It is hard for us who have lived our lives under the blessing of electricity to realize how very dark the nights were before Thomas Edison gave his work of genius to the world. But many men are still living in a candlelight world, refusing to take advantage of the light of the gospel. "In whom the god of this world hath blinded the minds of them who believe not, lest the light of the glorious gospel of Christ, who is the image of God, should shine unto them" (2 Corinthians 4:4).

But if they will in faith reach out to Jesus, their lives will be flooded with light. "Thy word is a lamp unto my feet, and a light unto my path," David cried in Psalm 119:105. It is only as we study the Word of God, "rightly dividing the word of truth" (2 Timothy 2:15) that we can come out of the darkness of fear and the fear of darkness and truly walk in the light of Jesus Christ.

FOOD FOR THOUGHT
1. *Were you afraid of the dark as a child? Why?*
2. *Are you now? Have any other fears been retained from childhood? List them.*
3. *How can you conquer such fears?*
4. *List Scriptures to help you. Memorize them.*

Chapter 5
Fear of Men's Faces

The clouds you so much dread
are big with mercy and will break
with blessings on your head!
    —author unknown

One day a man appeared at Marcia's door and asked to use her phone. Something about him kept her from permitting him to enter. She realized she had made him angry, but she felt her intuition was correct—perhaps it was direct guidance from the Holy Spirit. Some hours later she heard a strange crackling sound outside and found her home had been set on fire. She did not actually see the man return, but neighbors had seen a car like his in the area at the time of the fire. Marcia stood by helplessly and watched in horror as her house burned to the ground.

I saw her a year later and found her rejoicing in the fact that her new home would soon be ready. "Are you afraid to move back into your house?" I asked her. "Oh, no," she replied. "God has taken all fear from my heart. I know that he protected me from that evil man that day, and he will keep me from harm in the future."

We cannot live in the paralysis of fear. Had not Marcia been a Christian and sure of God's protecting love, she might have been enslaved to a fear of man. But her faith triumphed over her fear, and she is looking confidently into the future. "For God hath not given us the spirit of fear, but of power, and of love, and of a sound mind" (2 Timothy 1:7).

Some of the earliest Bible verses I can remember being taught in Sunday school concerned fear. "What time I am afraid, I will trust in thee" (Psalm 56:3). "The Lord is my light and my salvation; whom shall I fear? The Lord is the strength of my life; of whom shall I be afraid?" (Psalm 27:1).

Of course, the fear of man can be a healthy fear—as long as it means having due respect for man, realizing that he is made in the image of God. Just as fear (reverence) is due the Trinity (God the Father, God the Son, and God the Holy Ghost), reverence (respect) is owed by man to man in his trichotomy (spirit, mind, and body).

When we show a lack of respect for a man's spirit, mind, or body, we are also being disrespectful to God, because man is the work of God's hands, the crown of his creation. We should respect men and women as God's handiwork, but we should not be afraid of them. We see both of these in the following Scriptures:

"Ye have heard that it was said by them of old, Thou shalt not kill and whosoever shall kill shall be in danger of judgment; but I say unto you that whosoever is angry with his brother without a cause shall be in danger of judgment; and whosoever shall say to his brother, Raca, shall be in danger of the council; but whosoever shall say, Thou fool, shall be in danger of hell fire. Therefore, if thou bring thy gift to the altar, and there rememberest that thy brother hath anything against thee, leave there thy gift before the altar, and go thy way; first be reconciled to thy brother, and then come and offer thy gift.'' (Matthew 5:21-24)

"Fear not them who kill the body." (Matthew 10:28)

So that we may boldly say, The Lord is my helper, and I will not fear what man shall do unto me. (Hebrews 13:6)

One implication of the first passage is that we sometimes suffer from a fear of man because of poor dealings with the specific person we fear. If we have not been upright in our relationship, we may dread seeing the one we have injured or slandered. This situation requires not only courage, but confession, and in some instances retribution.

None of us is exempt from the fear of man at one time or another. An infant trusts his father and mother with their soft voices. But if a stranger speaks to him in a loud voice, the infant may shake with fear.

If not controlled, fear in a small child can grow into a phobia that will cripple his progress in life. He may be afraid of his teachers and fail in school. He may be afraid to apply for a position, or may suffer from such a fear of his boss that he is unable to function properly on the job.

I suffered from a fear of my first boss that caused me to be tongue-tied and unable to express myself before him. When he looked over my shoulder, I made typing errors I would not have made otherwise.

Fortunately for me, at this time in my life I sat under the expository Bible teaching of a fine minister who taught me that the ground is level at the foot of the cross; God is no respecter of persons. "He maketh his sun to rise on the evil and on the good, and sendeth rain on the just and on the unjust" (Matthew 5:45).

My godly pastor taught us that we are equal in God's sight; regardless of position, wealth, fame, or power, all men are the same in God's eyes. Since then I have endeavored to see men as God sees them, and the fear of men's faces has left me. I know that God is not impressed with all the riches or possessions a man has. Rather, God "looketh on the heart" (1 Samuel 16:7) and judges man by what is inside, in his inner spirit. I can converse as easily with the rich landowner as with the TV repairman, without fear of either—all because of God's work within me.

A humor columnist once wrote that when she had to interview upper-echelon individuals, she imagined them wearing long woolen underwear—the kind with buttons down the front and a buttoned split in the back. She was thus able to query the interviewee without her knees trembling or her hands growing clammy.

One of the most formidable positions I have ever held was as a recording secretary to a twenty-man board of a mission. These men were all better educated than I was, and this was at a time when women were relegated to the back of the bus in the business world. I tried to bolster my ego by reminding myself I had been an honor student in school, had won prizes for my writing both in poetry and prose, and was married to a distinguished professor who held an administrative position of importance in the world of education. But as the time approached for the minute taking, I suffered from what was definitely a fear

of man. I took the suggestion of the humorist and over-
came the difficult situation by writing a free-verse poem
to ease my tension.

I was afraid of their faces
men's faces, heavy jowled
stern faces with straight-
line lips that screamed
though silent "I hold a Ph.D.
from Princeton!" "Mine is from Yale."
"And I . . . am a Harvard man."
    "How can you spend ten hours,
    one lone female secretary
    with such an imposing body?"
    my inner self asked my inner self.
My imagination (sometimes an unsanctified
unholy thing) played guardian angel:
The round table turned into a pot-
bellied stove and the board members
one by one Norman Rockwelled
into a scene suited for a Saturday Evening Post
cover. Gone were the gray herringbone
suits and before my eyes each man
stood in woolen longies, buttoned
tightly down the front,
but split-backed so that they kept
their backs to the stove for modesty's sake.
At the sight of the chairman
of the board wearing red long johns
all fear left me
a smile danced
on my lips as I poised
my pen to write down
the motions of the all-day meeting.

God has given us a sense of humor, and it often comes
to our rescue in the face of what could develop into a
major problem. The poem was my attempt to remind

myself that there are some things that are basic to all
men: eating, sleeping, dressing, undressing, the ground
at the foot of the cross.

If we're not to fear people, how should we feel toward
them? What are the alternatives?

With Will Rogers I can say, "I have never known a
man (or woman) I did not like." Admittedly, some have
fallen short of my expectations. But we would probably
be more sympathetic toward everyone if we understood
the struggles or sorrows they face.

Realizing when you meet a stranger, "This is a unique
person God made," will develop genuine interest in
each individual you meet. Everyone needs the encouragement *you* can give. Give it unstintingly. A
teacher once said he treated each of his students with
respect since he did not know but one of them might be
another Martin Luther.

We can be glad God does not judge men the way we
do—by the cars they drive, by the homes in which they
live, by the clothes they wear, or the style of their hair, or
the color of their eyes or skin. "But the Lord said unto
Samuel, Look not on his countenance [referring to
Eliab], or on the height of his stature, because I have
refused him; for the Lord seeth not as man seeth; for man
looketh on the outward appearance, but the Lord looketh
on the heart" (1 Samuel 16:7).

God's Word tells us that every man is "naked and
opened unto the eyes of him with whom we have to do"
(Hebrews 4:13). God is unimpressed by the Saks Fifth
Avenue label on our clothing or the Florsheim imprint on
our shoes. He is more concerned about our being clothed
in the righteousness of his Son, which we receive as a

gift when we commit our lives to Christ. Ephesians 6:13-18 describes this clothing:

> Take unto you the whole armor of God, that ye may be able to withstand in the evil day, and having done all, to stand. Stand, therefore, having your loins girded about with truth, and having on the breastplate of righteousness, and your feet shod with the preparation of the gospel of peace; above all, taking the shield of faith, with which ye shall be able to quench all the fiery darts of the wicked. And take the helmet of salvation, and the sword of the Spirit, which is the word of God; praying always with all prayer and supplication in the Spirit.

When we are fully clothed in the righteousness of Christ, we can then have proper respect for man as God's created being and be free of the fear of men. We know that all men were made by God, and no men exist that were not made by him. Furthermore, no man can earn Heaven through his own works. Jesus said, "I am the way, the truth, and the life; no man cometh unto the Father, but by me" (John 14:6). We must all go through the Door, Jesus Christ (John 10:7), on our knees.

A perfect love toward God and toward his creature (man) results in a right attitude toward man and a life that is free from the bondage of unhealthy fear. "There is no fear in love, but perfect love casteth out fear, because fear hath torment. He that feareth is not made perfect in love" (1 John 4:18).

FOOD FOR THOUGHT

1. *Do you fear man? Why?*
2. *What thought processes can help you overcome such fear?*
3. *Does realizing that all men share a common denominator help to abolish your fear of men?*

4. *Memorize a verse that makes you realize that the ground is level at the foot of the cross.*

Chapter 6
Fear of the Unknown

Though my soul may set in darkness, it
will rise in perfect light.
I have loved the stars too fondly to be
fearful of the night.
        —Sarah Williams,
        "The Old Astronomer"

Fear of the unknown plagues everyone at some time or other. We might say it is the fear in which many other fears have their roots. We see it evidenced in small children who are afraid to wade in a pool for the first time, or to ride a pony, or to ride a train or elevator or escalator.

If this fear is not resolved in childhood, it may carry over into adult life and make a Caspar Milquetoast out of a man or a nervous Nellie out of a woman. (In case you are too young to know who Caspar Milquetoast was, he was a comic strip character who was more mouse than man and was portrayed as a timid, chinless person who was afraid of not only *his* shadow, but everyone else's also.)

Some couples live all their married life in rented apartments, afraid to move out on faith into an unknown area (geographically and financially) and to purchase a home. At the end of their working years, they find themselves with nothing but a stack of rent receipts when they could have been building financial security for their old age. Some men stay at an unfulfilling job with small pay because they are afraid to launch out into the business world. Success and growth are always built on an element of risk—a risk of the unknown.

Beside me one year in the Orange Bowl Parade bleachers was an attractive woman of about fifty who suffered from a deep fear of the unknown. Separated from her husband of thirty years, because of his alcoholism, now planning on taking some college courses in preparation for returning to the business world (she had not been a secretary since before her marriage), her fears were intense. I shared with her that there are no unknowns to God; he knows the end from the beginning. We may be surprised at the sudden turns our lives take, but the illnesses, the losses we suffer, the disappointments in people—these are never a surprise to him. He has a plan for our lives, and we should "commit [our] way unto the Lord; trust also in him, and he shall bring it to pass" (Psalm 37:5).

Nothing ever happens in our lives without God's foreknowledge. In Psalm 139, we are assured that God's all-seeing eye never sleeps. "Thou knowest my downsitting and mine uprising; thou understandest my thought afar off." God knows all about everything we face. He understands our most severe trials and our most ecstatic triumphs. Whatever challenge we experience—a demanding boss, a particularly strong-willed child, the death of a loved one—we need not wonder what to do or fear what the future will bring. God is sufficient for our every unknown; we can trust him fully. As others have written—

Faith is the daring of the soul to go farther than it can see. (William Newton Clarke)

All I have seen teaches me to trust the Creator for all I have not seen. (Ralph Waldo Emerson)

The devil hasn't armies enough to capture one saint of God who dares to trust him. (Benjamin de Jong)

The woman seated next to me at the parade later threatened to commit suicide. The fear of the unknown was more than she could handle. She had not stocked her spiritual pantry and when the trial came, she was Mother Hubbard with not even a bone. We either control our circumstances, or our circumstances will control us. Only our belief in Christ (or actually the Christ in whom we believe) can get us through such a time of stress.

Rather than fearing the unknown, we should fear and serve God. Faith is always fear's antidote. "Blessed is the man who walketh not in the counsel of the ungodly, nor standeth in the way of sinners, nor sitteth in the seat of the scornful. But his delight is in the law of the Lord; and in his law doth he meditate day and night" (Psalm 1:1, 2). "Serve the Lord with fear, and rejoice with trembling. . . . Blessed are all they who put their trust in him" (Psalm 2:11, 12).

Knowing, with more than a casual head-knowledge but with a deep heart-knowledge, that he who guides the stars in their paths is also guiding us can remove the fear of the unknown from our lives. "A man's heart deviseth his way, but the Lord directeth his steps" (Proverbs 16:9). God has endowed man with freedom of choice. God did not want a world of robots. Rather, he desired that men and women would *choose* to love and follow him. He never forces anyone into being a believer.

Francis Thompson portrays God, in what has been called the greatest lyric ever written in the English language, as the "Hound of Heaven." The hound is eternally on the scent of the hunted, for their good. We may be grateful that he is a God of mercy and perseverance who seeks out his children when they turn away from him. "I don't believe a loving God would sentence a man to Hell," some say. God never sent anyone to Hell. When an individual turns his back on God's gift of salvation through Jesus Christ, he turns himself toward eternal separation from God. But the choice is his.

Paul's sermon on Mars Hill began, "Ye men of Athens, I perceive that in all things ye are very religious. For as I passed by, and beheld your devotions, I found an altar with this inscription, TO THE UNKNOWN GOD. Whom, therefore, ye ignorantly worship, him declare I unto you" (Acts 17:22, 23). When Paul went on to talk about the resurrection of the dead, some mocked, some said, "We will hear thee again of this matter." But "certain men joined him, and believed, among whom were Dionysius, the Areopagite, and a woman named Damaris, and others with them" (vv. 33, 34).

The unknown God (a crutch for those afraid of the unknown?) became known to these certain individuals because they believed. They were now free from the orgies of the Epicureans in the temple of Diana—a religion they abandoned as a hopeless search by reason for truth, whose advocates gave their lives to the seeking of pleasure.

We find many persons in our day ascribing to a religion of hedonism—"eat, drink, and be merry, for tomorrow we die." It is a superficial merriment in which there exists no real joy. Joy, antidote for fear of the unknown, is supernatural and can exist only in the believer who has had the unknown god revealed to him through the person of Jesus Christ, his Son.

The marker with the inscription TO THE UNKNOWN GOD may still be seen by visitors to Mars Hill. Paul's message is needed today. As long as men cannot fill the void in their lives, they will continue to suffer from a fear of the unknown. They cannot say with Paul, "I know whom I have believed and am persuaded that he is able to keep that which I have committed unto him against that day" (2 Timothy 1:12).

Trust in the God who has revealed himself and who can be known personally brings hope and help to an uncertain future.

When Lydia was six years old (in Austria, during World War II), her father was killed by the Russians. Her mother and the four little girls, ranging from six years to six weeks, were herded into an open cattle car and taken to a series of flea-infested concentration camps. For many months they subsisted on a poor diet of pea soup (with black bugs left in the soup for added protein).

In addition to the anxiety over the children's welfare, there was always the danger of rape by the soldiers, Russian or German. Each morning brought a fear of what would happen in that day to the small brood. Had the mother not had faith in God, she could not have lived through the inhuman prison camps and their debasement.

God was in every unknown for Lydia and her sisters. Today she is a grown woman living with her husband and children in southern Florida and full of praise to God for the way he protected and delivered her and her family. She is a living testimony to Isaiah 35:4—''Say to those who are of a fearful heart, Be strong, fear not; behold, your God will come with vengeance, even God, with a recompense; he will come and save you.'' The future of Lydia's family had been dark, but God cared for them in an amazing way.

Today is the tomorrow we worried about yesterday, and God is here!

Perhaps as much as 90 percent of the things we worry about never happen. That leaves 10 percent to put our faith to the test. What is your greatest concern for tomorrow? That you might not have enough money for your needs in your old age? That you might have cancer? That your children might neglect you when you are old? Place yourself and your tomorrow with its unknown problems safely in the hands of God. God is truly in every tomorrow; he is the great problem-solver. There are no unknowns to him.

Are you living in a prison of fear of the unknown? God promises ''to bring out the prisoners from the prison, and those who sit in darkness out of the prison house'' (Isaiah 42:7). And, ''When thou passest through the waters, I will be with thee; and through the rivers, they shall not overflow thee; when thou walkest through the fire, thou shalt not be burned'' (Isaiah 43:2). If we walk beside a God like that, why should we fear anything?

Secular psychology says man's primary goal is to be happy. Nowhere in the Bible do we find happiness to be the main purpose for man, but rather the underlying purpose is to please God at every moment.

The Apostle Paul was an example of this:

As we were allowed of God to be put in trust with the gospel, even so we speak; not as pleasing men but God, who trieth our hearts. (1 Thessalonians 2:4)

The person who, like Paul, has as his goal pleasing God has reached a level of spiritual maturity that will not only free him from fear of the unknown, but also bring him success in his personal relationships, be it student/teacher, husband/wife, parent/child, employer/employee. Relationships constitute the core of our lives. Whenever secondary relationships falter, it is because one or both persons involved is not maintaining a strong relationship with God. When a man earnestly seeks to please God, he will find in most instances that his fellowship with men improves too.

When a man's ways please the Lord, he maketh even his enemies to be at peace with him. (Proverbs 16:7)

If we walk in the light, as he is in the light, we have fellowship one with another, and the blood of Jesus Christ, his Son, cleanseth us from all sin. (1 John 1:7)

A story is told of an itinerant Southern black preacher who preached one sermon wherever he went. His topic was, "Let this mind be in you, which was also in Christ Jesus" (Philippians 2:5). What an important message for his day and for ours. There is no unhealthy fear in the mind that is truly Christlike. But when fear vanishes, the vacuum that remains must be flooded with faith, a faith that is the product of his glorious light, a faith in which there is no darkness at all, a faith that cries with Paul, "I have learned, in whatever state I am, in this to be content" (Philippians 4:11). For "godliness with contentment is great gain" (1 Timothy 6:6).

Faith is not an accomplishment of man, but a gift from God. When Jesus asked Peter, "Who say ye that I am?" Peter answered, "Thou art the Christ, the Son of the living God." Our Lord told him, "Flesh and blood hath not revealed it unto thee, but my Father, who is in heaven" (Matthew 16:17). To know that Christ is the Messiah is truly a gift from God the Father.

We can trust God with all of our tomorrows, for he is "the same yesterday, and today, and forever" (Hebrews 13:8). Our future holds no surprises to God, and knowing him well is to have no fear of the unknown.

In a nursing home which I often visit, there is a sharp contrast in the people who live there. Some murmur and complain about every little thing. Nothing satisfies them. They are without spiritual perception. They do not really know God. They are living out their old age as they lived all of the other years of their lives—without God. There are some, however, whose faces radiate peace and joy. One such person said to me, "I am so grateful to God for letting me be here where I have my food prepared for me and someone to wheel me around in my wheelchair. I can no longer care for myself and I am glad to be where there is someone to help take care of me."

She had learned, with Paul, to be content in whatever state she found herself. People do not sprout angel-wings in old age. They become just a little more of what they have always been. Complainers find even more to complain about. Those who have been used to meeting the day with a smile seem to smile a little more often in old age. How sad it is when one reaches eighty without a personal relationship with Jesus Christ. He alone can keep fear out of the believer's life. Without him, there is no hope, no hope at all.

FOOD FOR THOUGHT

1. *Do you suffer at times from a fear of the unknown? Why?*
2. *List a specific instance where a fear of the unknown has inhibited you.*
3. *Were you able to free yourself from such a fear? If so, how did you do it?*
4. *If you conquered such a fear in the past, do you think you will be able to in the future? Why or why not?*
5. *Choose a Scripture that can be of help to you in conquering a fear of the unknown. Memorize it.*

Chapter 7
Fear of Suffering and the Scalpel

If this year I should be disturbed or
molested in the exercise of my ministry,
if I should be silenced, or otherways
suffer for well-doing, I commit the
keeping of my soul to God as a faithful
Creator; depending upon him to guide me
in my call to suffer, and to make clear,
and to preserve me from perplexing snares;
depending upon him to support and comfort
me under my sufferings, and to bring glory
to himself out of them, and then welcome his
whole will.
        —Matthew Henry (1662-1714),
        from his diary, New Year's Day, 1704

A number of years ago my doctor asked me to see him
and to come prepared to check into the hospital if need
be. His phone call was a follow-up on an examination
made two days earlier. A sudden fear gripped me. What
had the biopsy revealed? Did I have cancer? Would I
need surgery?

I can remember staring into a shop window on Chicago's Michigan Avenue after I left the doctor's office, wishing I could buy something special for two small daughters. "An ectopic pregnancy. Immediate surgery." The doctor had given me no options. I knew it was a serious operation; there was grave danger of hemorrhage. I wondered if I would ever see my children again. A feeling of weakness made my feet unsure, weakness caused by fear.

An hour later as I walked into the room assigned me at Michael Reese Hospital, I caught a view of the lake from the window. The window framed Lake Michigan as though it were a picture hanging on the wall. I remembered how Jesus loved to walk beside the Sea of Galilee. A feeling of peace enveloped me. "Thank you, God," my quieted heart shouted. Gone was all fear. I knew God would be with me whatever happened. Life or death was all right, for God was in charge.

I introduced myself to my roommate and discovered she was a Jewess who lived in the same apartment building as my mother in Oak Park. There were eight million people living in Chicago and its environs, but I knew this was no coincidence. God had some reason for bringing me to this hospital and to this room with this dear woman who was convulsed in pain from a slipped disc in her back. I told her I would pray for her.

She said, "I can't believe you! Here you are facing a serious operation, and you are perfectly calm and offering to pray for me!"

Later a nurse came in and commented, "You are a Christian, aren't you?"

"How ever could you tell?" I asked.

"If you did not know Christ, you could not possibly face so serious an operation with such complete calm—and no fear."

I went through the operation with the peace that passes all understanding in my heart. God did this within me.

I do not think of myself as a brave person. It had taken several nurses to hold me down when I had a tonsillectomy at the age of five, and that little child of five still lived deep within me. But here I was facing the greatest physical crisis of my life with complete calm. This absence of fear was not something I drummed up or dreamed up. It was a supernatural work of grace in my heart. "My grace is sufficient for thee" (2 Corinthians 12:9).

When we lived in St. Louis, our senior pastor John Hay and his wife, Sadie, lived in the apartment on the floor above us. One evening I called Pastor Hay to the phone we shared. I heard the tenseness in his voice as he called up to his wife, "Sadie, it's about Ian. He's in the hospital. There's been an accident."

Leaning over the railing from the landing, serene and lovely, Sadie said, "Remember, John, the Lord is in this too."

The Lord is in this too. The Lord *was* with thirteen-year-old Ian. He grew up to become a missionary to Nigeria and later director for the Sudan Interior Mission.

The Lord is in this too. The secret to facing an accident, an illness, an operation without fear is to remember that God is in every situation we face. We are the sheep of his pasture, and he will not let the lion of fear consume us. He wants us to enjoy the green pastures of his caring and to lie down beside the still waters of his presence.

In his book *Love Therapy,* Paul Morris writes about the psychologist who practiced paracaletic psychology (psychology led by the Holy Spirit). He recommended to a patient suffering from hypertension and insomnia that he recite the 23rd Psalm out loud eight times a day. This the man did. When he returned to the pastor-psychologist's study ten days later, he was a new man. All fear had left him. His blood pressure had returned to normal, and he was sleeping well through the night—because he knew the Lord was indeed his shepherd and that he truly did not want. He had no needs God could not supply.

We can know about the Bible, and even learn many verses, but until we practically apply it to our lives on a daily basis, we are apt to suffer the same fears that plague unbelievers.

There is no greater boost in learning to live without fear than to know God and enjoy close fellowship with him. It is not sufficient to know about him. It is important to know him personally.

A fear of illness can be a healthy fear. It can persuade us to observe proper health rules, eat good food with an emphasis on vegetables, fruit, lean meats, dairy products and whole grains, and bypass refined sugars, flours, and junk foods. Such a reasonable fear may serve to help avoid tobacco, alcohol, and drugs or to have a physical checkup regularly. It may lead us into a proper exercise program. But when a wise concern for health turns into an unwise anxiety, it can make the individual a hypochondriac. Such anxiety springs from a lack of faith in God as the Great Physician "who healeth all thy diseases" (Psalm 103:3). "Be anxious for nothing," Paul writes, "but in everything, by prayer and supplication with thanksgiving, let your requests be made known unto God" (Philippians 4:6). This is not a suggestion, but a command.

I once knew a man who had such excessive concern for his health that he always came to church late so he could sit in a back pew or outside in the foyer, away from others. When his wife broke her pelvic bone, he took to his bed on a real or imagined illness and did not even visit her in the hospital. (The truth was, he was afraid he might pick up some disease in the hospital.) All of his precautions (including refusing to eat in a restaurant or to take public transportation) failed to add years to his life. He died before he reached seventy.

The "Be anxious for nothing" verse we quoted is followed by, "and the peace of God, which passeth all understanding, shall keep your hearts and minds through Christ Jesus" (Philippians 4:7). Physical and spiritual health often go together.

When my grandmother was taken to the hospital, she told me she was not afraid to die, for she knew she would be with Jesus; but she was afraid of the pain she might have to suffer before she was taken home. Pain is a strange and lonely island. It separates the sufferer from all that is around him. Although he may be surrounded by other people, the sufferer in the throes of his agony finds their faces blotted out and their voices inaudible.

Pain is generally borne alone, though in rare instances pain has been shared by a loved one. C. S. Lewis tells in one of his books of bearing his wife's pain as she lay dying from cancer. Whether he actually had this mystical experience or not, we have no way of knowing. Perhaps his pain was so great, he thought he was bearing her pain for her.

Philip Yancey has given us a classic study of pain in his book, *Where Is God When It Hurts?* (Zondervan, 1977). It may be a bit easier to understand than the book on the same subject by C. S. Lewis, *The Problem of Pain*, though the latter is valuable reading.

Yancey's book discusses several individuals and their personal bouts with pain (among them Joni Eareckson, the quadriplegic; Brian Sternberg; and a minister tortured in Dachau). His conclusion from his five years of researching pain is: *we can cope with pain when we remember the sufferings of our Lord.* As we relate our individual pain to his suffering and actually have fellowship with him in his sufferings (he bore the pain and sorrows of the world he created), we receive the grace to endure whatever physical or mental suffering is ours to experience.

Some persons faced with illness and suffering become angry with God for sending or permitting the affliction. There is an old cliche, "when you cannot beat them, join them." We know God will triumph in the end, and it is far better to be on his side than to bitterly turn against him and fight a lone battle in the dark.

Jim Elliot, one of the five missionaries martyred by the Auca Indians, recognized this truth when he wrote: "He is no fool who gives what he cannot keep to gain what he cannot lose."

Perhaps your name, like Job's, has been brought before the throne by Satan when he comes before God. Is suffering your private testing? Remember,

There hath no temptation taken you but such as is common

to man; but God is faithful, who will not permit you to be tempted above that ye are able, but will, with the temptation, also make the way to escape, that ye may be able to bear it. (1 Corinthians 10:13)

In other words, God will not permit us to be tested beyond what we can endure; he will give us the grace to endure to the end. Faith in God's sovereignty frees us from fear of illness and gives us the assurance that although we may be called upon to endure suffering, he will never leave or forsake us.

Studies have shown that persons with Christian faith recover more rapidly from operations and illnesses. A recent study by Dr. Berton H. Kaplan and Dr. Curtis G. Hames, professors of epidemiology at the University of North Carolina (Public Health), shows that there is a consistent association between fear and attendance at church. Their study, published in the *Journal of Behavioral Medicine*, focused on the effects of just one factor—church attendance—on the blood pressure of 355 men in Evans County, Georgia. Involvement in a church contributes three things that regulate fear, according to the two professors:

1. The rituals of religion are comforting. They are a stable, seldom changing factor in this age of unpredictability.
2. There is a form of extended family in churches which supports the individual. He or she doesn't have the feeling of being alone. There are always others there to help. Dr. Hames states, "People who attend church frequently have lower blood pressures than people who do not. Religion provides a social, psychological and emotional support. A person with a good religious life doesn't have the anxiety that if something happens to him, he'll be totally alone."
3. There are models in religious teachings of how to cope

with despair, fear, anxiety, and other such moods. Because of his faith in God, a religious person grounded in these teachings will not lose hope.

Paul recognized the importance of church attendance when he exhorted, "Not forsaking the assembling of yourselves together" (Hebrews 10:25). Such neglect has a high toll on the bridge of backsliding and loss of well-being.

Faith heals; when the mind is free from fear, the body can function more readily. God has built great healing ability into our bodies. Medical doctors cannot heal; they can simply prescribe medicine to aid the body in doing its own work of healing. Look up the following verses on healing:

Psalm 67:2—"thy saving health among all nations"
Psalm 103:3—"who healeth all thy diseases"
Isaiah 53:5—"with his stripes we are healed"
Malachi 4:2—"with healing in his wings"
Acts 14:9—"perceiving that he had faith to be healed"
1 Peter 2:24—"by whose stripes ye were healed"

As believers, we know that God only permits those illnesses, accidents, and operations to come into our lives that will prove the "trial of your faith [to be] much more precious than of gold that perisheth, [that we] might be found unto praise and honor and glory at the appearing of Jesus Christ" (1 Peter 1:7).

No matter what we face, he is the same. "Unto you, therefore, who believe he is precious" (1 Peter 2:7).

Is he precious to you? Do you have every confidence in him? Do you know he shields your life with his precious blood and only that which he can use for your good can penetrate that shield?

With Sarah Hay and the multitude of saints who have gone before, you can know freedom from fear and say in the face of danger, "The Lord is in this too."

FOOD FOR THOUGHT
1. *Do you sincerely believe that no matter what happens in your life, "the Lord is in this too"?*
2. *How can Romans 8:28 apply to accidents and illnesses as well as to periods of good health and well-being?*
3. *Can anything harm the Christian unless God first permits it?*
4. *List some biblical promises of God's care. Memorize them.*

Chapter 8

Fear of Growing Old or Being Alone

When I look Life in the eyes
Grown calm and very coldly wise
Life will have given me the Truth,
And taken in exchange—my youth.
> —Sara Teasdale,
> "Wisdom"

Orientals give the seat of honor to the elderly. But we Americans give our attention to the small child and his antics, the teenager and his accomplishments in athletics or music. We ask youth what are their ambitions, their goals. Rarely is the older person asked, "What have you accomplished in life? What are you doing now? What do you hope to accomplish before you die?" Middle age and thereon is considered over the hill.

In its healthy state, a fear of old age can cause a person to plan for his or her retirement years. In addition to financial considerations, such planning should involve interests that have been cultivated in youth or adulthood (reading, travel, gardening, church work, Bible study, boating, fishing, etc.). Hobbies such as bird watching, shell collecting, rock collecting, as well as interests in the arts, music, painting, history, macrame, crewel work, knitting, crocheting, can help to make old age (in fact, any age) fascinating.

I was recently in the home of a friend who is a recognized sculptor and painter. The demands for her work are many. Retirement is not in her vocabulary. Her husband is retired from his field of activity, and what could have been a difficult situation has proved to be rewarding. He frames her art, hunts for wood for unique frames, crates her work for shipping, sees that it is properly mailed. He hauls her work to museums where she frequently exhibits, and then hauls it home again. In addition to supportive measures in his wife's work, he spends time working on latchwork rugs and has made some beautiful ones for wall hangings.

A wide range of interests in early adulthood can guarantee an interesting old age. Persons who are keenly alive at seventy and eighty are those persons who have kept a lively interest in everything about them.

If you suffer inwardly from a fear of growing old, it would be well to carefully observe those older people within your circle of acquaintances. What are the characteristics of those older people you admire? What are the traits you dislike? Your list might look something like this:

Undesirable characteristics	Admirable characteristics
feebleness	healthy body
whining, complaining	positive approach to life
lack of appreciation	gratefulness to be alive

always wants to be served
lack of interest in others
selfishness
no interest in hobbies
no interest in world affairs
no interest in family life
no interest in community
fretfulness
negativism
slovenly attire
lack of religious faith
no interest in reading
vegetablelike state

thankful for small favors
interest in other people
helpfulness
interest in world around them
interest in voting
interest in church
informed on issues
sense of humor
tolerance
neatness
strong faith in Christ
interest in reading
refusal to give in to dull
    existence

To the happy octogenarian, old age is not an ending: life goes on, and he is looking forward to the Great Adventure. If the unbeliever can see no further than the grave, no wonder his days are dismal, his talk negative, and his outlook gloomy. For the older person owning faith in God and his Son, death is but an open door to a higher realm of living.

A fear of old age has cocooned within it many other fears: fear of poverty, fear of ill health, fear of dying, fear of loneliness, fear of the unknown. A named fear seldom exists in isolation.

When one looks at old age as a decade or two of living without one's mate (which is true of more than 80 percent of all older people) and enduring severe aches and disabilities, the picture is apt to contain a very real element of fear and dread. But when old age is seen as living one day at a time, facing only the problems of that one day, with the firm realization that God will give the grace to face whatever may come, old age can be lived triumphantly and with joy. "Be, therefore, not anxious about tomorrow; for tomorrow will be anxious for the things of itself. Sufficient unto the day is its own evil" (Matthew 6:34).

Old age can be blessed with wisdom and judgment that youth lacks. I was in the home of a friend one day when her sixteen-year-old daughter came home in a gala mood—she had just obtained her driver's license. She dashed out to the garage, hopped into the family car, and backed out of the drive. But there her happy mood ended as her rear bumper crashed into a car parked across the street. She had had driver's education in school and had passed with flying colors. She had excellent health, good vision, good hearing, and all of the attributes of youth. But she lacked one thing—experience. This prized attribute only comes with time.

Don't misunderstand me—I'm not trying to minimize the difficulties of old age. For the most part, we are on limited incomes, usually Social Security and the interest from whatever investments we have had the forethought to make. We are usually aware of a lack of physical endurance. Often we are forced to live within physical limitations imposed upon us by poor eyesight or hearing, or weakness of vital organs (poor circulation, high blood pressure, arthritis, etc.).

In old age, as in any other phase of life, we must choose between being content or complaining, serving others or serving self, being sweet or sour. And some of us choose the latter. We wear perpetual frowns; we are crab-apple people.

But some among the crab apples are golden delicious despite the strong winds of old age. Such a person is radiant and full of life. This person has learned to say with Paul, "I have learned, in whatever state I am, in this to be content" (Philippians 4:11). And, "In everything give thanks; for this is the will of God in Christ Jesus concerning you" (1 Thessalonians 5:18). Obedience to or neglect of this command means the difference between the beauty of a golden delicious apple or the bitterness of a crab apple.

Thought patterns are first level paths and then deep rutted lanes that are hard to change. But through the grace of God they can be changed. With his help you can remove the negative from your life. Start today. Memorize Scriptures that will help you live positively and you will not fear old age. You know that God will be in your old age and that you can trust him to never leave or forsake you (Hebrews 13:5).

Are you afraid you may someday be blind? Do not fear. Instead fill your reading hours with inspirational readings now. Memorize passages of Scripture that are especially meaningful to you—Psalm 23, Psalm 91, Isaiah 53, John 14, John 1, Romans 8. Memorize entire chapters rather than verses scattered here and there.

Nothing can give stability and courage to old age like the memorization of God's Word. One dear woman who had been a devout Christian all of her life lost her sight some months before she died. She would lie on her bed, her face glowing with an inner radiance that lessened her wrinkles and made her beautiful as she recited aloud the many verses of Scripture she had memorized in her seeing days. She was physically blind but spiritually healthy and full of joy.

In the mobile court in Florida where I spend my winters, I have good opportunity to observe the differences in the way people face old age. Two examples will suffice. One man, who has lost his wife, lives alone and finds his greatest "comfort" in his bottle. He told one neighbor, "I would like to die. I have no reason to be on this earth and to be eating food that is needed by someone younger." How sad! He has no fellowship with the Lord or with people. He has taken what to him is the easy way out.

Another man also became an alcoholic, but his wife channeled him into a church where there was a special group to help alcoholics and other drug addicts. The man soon made a commitment to the Lord, and his life was entirely changed. He now goes regularly to church with his wife and participates in the life of the community. Christ made all the difference.

The Savior can remove the fear of old age from either the younger or older person, and he does it through the Word of God. But like food, it is of no benefit until it is eaten and eaten regularly. As Jeremiah said, "Thy words were found, and I did eat them, and thy word was unto me the joy and rejoicing of mine heart" (15:16).

Whenever I autograph one of my books for someone, I write the reference 2 Timothy 1:7 under my name. That verse says, "For God hath not given us the spirit of fear, but of power, and of love, and of a sound mind." Once a woman came up to me after a service and shared how much my book of poetry had meant to her. "But," she continued, "more than any of your poems, the verse you wrote under your autograph helped me the most."

God is not behind our fear; he asks us to trust him. Fear thrives when faith is absent. "There is no fear in love, but perfect love casteth out fear, because fear hath punishment [or torment]. He that feareth is not made perfect in love" (1 John 4:18). God loves us; so why should we fear?

Another implication of this is that as we grow in our love for God, we will know freedom from the fear of old age. In addition to your own individual Bible study, join · a Bible study group where you will feel free to ask questions and have your spiritual needs met.

How can we overcome a fear of old age? By realizing that our times are in God's hands. Whether life or death is ours, he is in control. Whether we die at the proverbial three score and ten or live to be a hundred, his choice for us is the right one. If we are slated for a long life, we can safely trust him to see us through those days that the preacher in Ecclesiastes refers to as "evil days": "remember now thy Creator in the days of thy youth, while the evil days come not, nor the years draw near when thou shalt say, I have no pleasure in them" (Ecclesiastes 12:1).

The fear of loneliness often accompanies the fear of old age. Sometimes this fear keeps the person constantly on the go to meetings, or parties, or bridge games until he finds himself in a vacuum in which is no happiness. A balance between being alone and being with people is essential to the well-adjusted life. As with the fear of old age, the fear of loneliness can be conquered only by knowing God, realizing who he is, and having a proper relationship with him. Realizing and practicing the presence of God is the way to lose the fear of loneliness.

The old hymn says, "No, never alone! No, never alone! He promised never to leave me, never to leave me alone." God is true to his promises; he cannot lie.

What shall separate us from the love of Christ? . . . For I am persuaded that neither death, nor life . . . nor any other creation, shall be able to separate us from the love of God, which is in Christ Jesus, our Lord. (Romans 8:35, 38, 39)

God will not only be a Friend to you himself, but will bring others into your life to dispel your loneliness. God saw Adam's aloneness and made a help meet (fit) for him. God knows what is best for you, whether a mate or a close friend. He is aware of your need for fellowship and will, if you look to him to supply your need, position you where you will find your life enriched with fulfilling friendships.

In my mobile court is a man who lost his wife several years ago. He is excruciatingly lonely, but refuses to participate in any of the games in the clubhouse or in the fellowship of a church. "None are so blind as they who will not see" could be paraphrased, "None are so lonely as they who refuse to make friends."

Friendships can be even more important in old age than they are in youth. Learn to be a good friend now, and you will have plenty of friends then. As we learned in the old Girl Scout song, "Make new friends, but keep the old. The new are silver, the old are gold." The old cliche is true: "Friendship is a two-way street." "A man who hath friends must show himself friendly" (Proverbs 18:24). If you nurture your friends as you would the plants in your south windows, you will find yourself rich in friendships.

Loving people is a sure cure for overcoming a fear of loneliness. As long as there are churches and people in them, you need never be lonely. It may cost you something—some of your time or money, some effort in being friendly, concern for the needs of the members—all of which add up to the giving of yourself as a friend.

One of the most satisfactory ways to lose a fear of loneliness is to seek out someone who is lonely and who needs a friend. When Jesus was asked, "Who is my neighbor?" he answered by telling a story about a man who concentrated on being a neighbor, who devoted his life to serving others, the good Samaritan. Jesus exemplified this spirit as well.

"The Son of man came, not to be ministered unto but to minister, and to give his life a ransom for many." (Mark 10:45)

An acquaintance of mine lost her husband some time ago and was almost overcome with the grief of the separation. I deliberately set out to help her overcome her grief and to adjust to her new life as a widow. The result: I made a good friend, one on whom I can depend for emotional support when I need her. When we try to meet someone else's need, without thinking about our own needs, we often find that the person we have tried to help has helped us. There are no one-way signs on Friendship Street.

However, we cannot fill this void in our lives entirely with people. We must first of all be filled with the presence of God; he must have first place in our lives. And when we give him our first love, we receive more love to pour out on other people.

Liking people, loving people is the key that locks the pasture gates so the poison weeds of fear cannot spread. The same key opens the golden gate of fulfillment in old age, leading to days filled with friends and above all with the presence of the Friend Divine. "There is a friend who sticketh closer than a brother" (Proverbs 18:24).

Paul Little once said, "In the final analysis, the Christian faith depends on the goodness of God. If he is good, we can safely follow him. If he is not, to follow him would be tragedy." He also said, "The will of God will never lead you where his grace cannot keep you." Whether in youth or old age, following him is the wisest thing we can do.

One thing God directs us to do is to prepare for our later years. This includes our financial life. A willingness to work in our younger years so that we can save and invest our earnings properly can insure an old age free from poverty and want. Statistics show that only two persons out of 100 are entirely financially independent by the age of retirement; 23 percent are able to support themselves with the aid of friends and relatives. The remaining 75 percent must be at some time or other on public aid (in addition to Social Security).

If you are not willing to face up to these figures and prefer to take an ostrich approach to life, you may find as you approach retirement that you have an accelerating fear of old age. Solomon wisely taught, "Go to the ant . . . consider her ways, and be wise" (Proverbs 6:6). Who has ever seen an ant loafing? They are always busy taking care of their communal needs and storing away morsels against the coming of winter.

Some who fear old age drive themselves ruthlessly, making every personal sacrifice to attain money and power. A mind without faith in God cannot help but subject itself to either the driving philosophy of the mammon-worshiping executive or the false philosophy of "eat, drink and be merry, for tomorrow we die." Both extremes are products of fear; both are the result of a lack of faith.

Biblically, 10 percent of our earnings belongs to the work of the Lord. As we honor him with our gifts, he blesses us abundantly.

Bring all the tithes into the storehouse, that there may be food in mine house, and test me now herewith, saith the Lord of hosts, if I will not open for you the windows of heaven, and pour out for you a blessing, that there shall not be room enough to receive it. (Malachi 3:10)

Malachi also recorded these encouraging words:

They that feared the Lord spoke often one to another; and the Lord hearkened, and heard it, and a book of remembrance was written before him for them that feared the Lord, and that thought upon his name. (3:16)

When we fear the Lord in our hearts, all other fears fall into proper perspective. The fear of old age will then neither cause us to foolishly eat, drink and be merry, nor to work day and night in a feverish attempt to save every cent against old age so that we cannot enjoy the early years of our lives. It does cause us to enrich our minds with inspirational writings and the Word of God, so we will not become impoverished in mind or body.

Victor Hugo wisely said, "Have courage for the great sorrows of life and patience for the small ones, and when you have laboriously accomplished your daily tasks, go to sleep in peace. God is awake."

God is indeed awake. He never slumbers or sleeps. Without his eternal vigilance, there would be no universe. It would fall apart or self-destruct without him. So when we commit our lives to him and live daily in the light of his presence, we can approach old age with a complete absence of fear. We can know he will take care of us, even though we often lack wisdom and make foolish mistakes. He loves us with an everlasting love that does not waiver or weaken. He is "the same yesterday, and today, and forever" (Hebrews 13:8).

I am often asked, "Do you mean you live in your big house—*alone?*" During the first weeks of my being alone in my house, I battled with fear. But I found that God gave me the grace I needed to live alone without fear. God was, and is, sufficient for my need.

One time I called the police when I heard a terrible crashing noise in an upstairs bedroom. The uniformed men went up the stairs cautiously, one with his hand on his pistol. Suddenly I heard uproarious laughter. Weakened by water from a leaky roof, the plaster on one of the bedroom ceilings had come down with a crash! (A burglar might have been less expensive than the cost of the ceiling repair!)

Was I afraid? Not really! I could not identify the loud noise and thought there might be an element of danger involved. But I was not quaking with fear; rather, I was possessed by a strange curiosity to find out what had made such a loud noise. God gets all the credit for this.

The *New International Version* translates 2 Timothy 1:7, the theme verse of this book, "For God did not give us a spirit of timidity, but a spirit of power, of love and of self-discipline."

Can there be such a thing as a timorous Christian? If faith is the substance of his life, how can he be fearful or timorous? Not so the apostles. The resurrection of Jesus changed them from cowards who sneaked away in fear from Gethsemane and Golgotha into fearless men witnessing to the truth of Christ's birth, death, and resurrection even when it meant their own martyrdom.

What is this "spirit of power" we are promised? It is the same power that transformed the lives of the apostles. It made courageous missionaries out of ordinary men such as Adoniram Judson, Hudson Taylor, Jim Elliot, Nate Saint, and many others.

Resurrection power endows men and women with the ability to live for God in whatever their calling, profession, or trade. It gives them courage to speak out against and to defy the evils of the day. The power of the gospel has always had its enemies, its Madalyn Murray O'Hairs, its Robert Ingersolls—atheists who are blinded by the "ruler of this world" and can neither see nor comprehend the glorious light of Jesus Christ. But unbelief can never conquer the Christian faith. Our Savior will care for us throughout our life, including old age.

FOOD FOR THOUGHT
1. *Do you fear old age for yourself? For someone you love?*
2. *What are you doing now to ensure a good old age?*
3. *What can you do for your parents to help them to adjust to these years?*
4. *Choose a beneficial Scripture and memorize it.*

Chapter 9
Fear of Doing and Daring

God's in his heaven,
All's right with the world.
  —Robert Browning,
  "Pippa Passes"

Sir Winston Churchill once said, "Courage is the first of human qualities because it is the quality which guarantees all others." A lack of this trait led Sidney Smith to observe, "A great deal of talent is lost to the world for want of a little courage. Every day sends to their graves obscure men whom timidity prevented from making a first effort."

I once fished with a friend in front of a rustic cabin in which lived a coarse, fishwife type of woman who taught me a great lesson in courage. Neither my friend nor I was the rugged outdoor type. Our lines often became ensnared on logs and other debris. The fishwife must have thought we were a couple of "poor city slickers." At one point, I caught a small sunfish, but it ended up in some high weeds. I was deathly afraid of whatever might be lurking in the weeds—especially snakes—and I cried out to our observer, "Will you please get my fish for me? I'm afraid to go into the high weeds."

A look of shocked contempt crossed the fishwife's face. "Do you mean you would ask someone else to do something you are afraid to do yourself?" Ashamed, I waded into the weeds and rescued my catch, well aware of the fishwife's curious eyes upon me. That day I learned to overcome a fear of walking in tall weeds. A humble, almost crude woman taught me to have courage, and a more real understanding of the Golden Rule.

Remember, the basis of our coping with fear is fearing the Lord. In a Bible class I attended recently, a woman asked, "Why does the Bible say we are supposed to fear God? I prefer to think of him as a God of love whom we do not need to fear."

Of course, "fear" not only means "painful emotion marked by alarm, dread, disquiet." It can also be "awe, profound reverence, especially for the Supreme Being." Awe and reverence for God do not cause alarm or disquiet. Rather, they bring a deep sense of quietude to the soul, a peace that passes understanding. Unless we have proper reverence for God, recognizing his sovereignty in our lives, we cannot truly comprehend his love for us and in turn love him the way he wants us to love him. He deserves to be loved before all others. Jesus said, "He that loveth father or mother more than me, is not worthy of me; and he that loveth son or daughter more than me, is not worthy of me" (Matthew 10:37). This can presumably be applied to any other human relationship—husband, wife, brother, sister, friend.

Job in his severe testings, losing first all that he possessed and then even his sons and daughters, and finally afflicted with sores all over his body, found that God had to come first in his affections. Encouraged by his wife to "Curse God, and die," Job instead prayed for his three "friends" who had only made his trials more difficult. Although he wondered in the depths of his soul why these trials had come upon him, because he feared God and recognized his sovereignty he was able to come out of his suffering victoriously. "And the Lord turned the captivity of Job, when he prayed for his friends; also the Lord gave Job twice as much as he had before" (Job 42:10).

In Job 19:25, 26 we find Job declaring, "For I know that my redeemer liveth, and that he shall stand at the latter day upon the earth; and though after my skin worms destroy this body, yet in my flesh shall I see God." What a declaration for Job to make, having no written Scriptures to assure him of the resurrection! "Though he slay me, yet will I trust in him!" (13:15) was the cry of his soul.

Yes, Job reverenced God, but he also had a "doing" kind of faith. He did not regain his vast possessions by sitting down and waiting for God to send him cattle and camels. He arose from the dust and ashes to start a new life. He probably traveled into adjacent lands to purchase the first cattle for his herds. It took a doing faith to see that they were properly cared for, so that they could multiply. A proper fear of the Lord never immobilizes; it activates and motivates.

Job buffeted Satan by daring to live dangerously for God. It takes faith to be "doers of the word and not hearers only'' (James 1:22). It takes faith to purchase a home and face high mortgage rates for years in the future, to purchase a new car, to enroll in college without knowing where the money will come from to pay tuition, to ask a girl to marry you knowing that you are financially responsible for her for the rest of her life, to have a family and risk having a child who is deformed and will need expensive medical care, to adopt a child not knowing what her heritage is, to start a business and risk failure, to plant a crop and risk the hazards of wind, hail and drought.

Why are we afraid to take action, to be doers? Perhaps we fear failure, or opposition, or inconvenience. Perhaps we just don't believe we can do what needs to be done, and often we can't—without God's help. It all comes back to faith.

When we hold a proper fear of God, we know that he is a loving God who honors faith. ''Without faith it is impossible to please him; for he that cometh to God must believe that he is, and that he is a rewarder of them that diligently seek him'' (Hebrews 11:6).

This verse in the great faith chapter of Hebrews 11 is followed by a listing of many Old Testament men and women who dared to live by their faith. They acted on their trust in God.

''By faith Noah, being warned of God of things not seen as yet, moved with fear, prepared an ark to the saving of his house, by which he condemned the world, and became heir of the righteousness which is by faith.'' Can you imagine the scorn on the faces of the townspeople who Noah and his sons faced daily as they worked for many years to complete the ark? Imagine the epithets that must have been hurled at them—"loons, idiots, morons, knuckleheads."

"By faith Abraham, when he was called to go out into a place which he should after receive for an inheritance, obeyed; and he went out, not knowing where he went." What a tremendous faith Abraham possessed—to leave his own land and travel into a vast unknown about which he had never read and had probably heard very little. Certainly there was no chamber of commerce to encourage him, no atlas to show him the way. But Abraham feared God and knew he could trust him to lead him and his family into a place of safety.

"Through faith also Sarah herself received strength to conceive seed, and was delivered of a child when she was past age, because she judged him faithful who had promised." Sarah was very human—she had laughed when Abraham told her about the angel's promise to him. But hers, too, was an action faith. She believed God would bring her through the rigors of childbirth in her old age. Her faith was rewarded by the birth of Isaac, through whom God blessed the world with many heirs of the faith and the bloodline of his own Son.

"By faith Isaac blessed Jacob and Esau concerning things to come."

"By faith Jacob, when he was dying, blessed both the sons of Joseph."

"By faith Joseph, when he died, made mention of the departing of the children of Israel and gave commandment concerning his bones."

"By faith Moses, when he was born, was hidden three months by his parents, because they saw he was a beautiful child, and they were not afraid of the king's command-

ment." Here we see the faith of Moses' parents, stem-
ming from a proper reverence for God, causing them to
not be afraid of the king's commandment. They were
serving a sovereign God whose command superseded an
earthly king's.

"By faith Moses, when he was come to years, refused
to be called the son of Pharaoh's daughter, choosing
rather to suffer affliction with the people of God than to
enjoy the pleasures of sin for a season, esteeming the
reproach of Christ greater riches than the treasures in
Egypt; for he had respect unto the recompense of the
reward."

"By faith the walls of Jericho fell down, after they
were compassed about seven days."

"By faith the harlot, Rahab, perished not with them
that believed not, when she had received the spies with
peace."

Here we see the miracle of God's grace. Not only did
he save Rahab from the enemy, but he forgave her sins.
She was "accepted in the Beloved" (Ephesians 1:6), and
became a part of the bloodline from which his only begotten Son would enter the world (see Matthew 1:5).

God places a high premium on faith. He can turn our
passive faith into an active one if we permit him to be
Lord and Sovereign King of our lives.

The author of Hebrews lists many heroes of the faith:
Gideon, Barak, Samson, Jephthah, David, Samuel, and
all the prophets. This list could be added to by many
names through the centuries, and by the names, perhaps
known only to God, of faithful men and women now
living on earth. You and I could add to this faith-list the
names of persons whom we know. Here is a partial list

made from my friends and family, and others of whom I have heard:

By faith Corrie ten Boom endured the atrocities of Ravensbruck prison and lived to write and tell of God's miraculous deliverance through those war years.

By faith Don Richardson wrote *Peace Child* and *Lords of the Earth*, thrilling stories of present-day missionary work in New Guinea.

By faith David Mains started the Circle Church in Chicago, where hundreds have found the Lord.

By faith his wife, Karen Mains, spends long hours writing books, having faith she will find a publisher, and that God will use her writing to challenge many in spiritual growth.

By faith Craig Burton entered Northern Baptist Seminary, believing God was leading him and would provide the money to complete his work on his Master's in Christian education.

By faith the staff of ministers of the First Presbyterian Church of North Palm, Florida, led their congregation to break ground for a much needed educational building. God will honor Pastor Jim Stout and his people.

By faith Bunny Davis led her alcoholic husband to a church group geared to working with persons on drugs and saw his life completely changed through Christ.

By faith the believers in Guatemala, ignoring their ruined homes, started immediately after the devastating earthquake to first rebuild their churches. The City of February 4 rises as a monument to the faith of these courageous believers, many of them still struggling to rebuild their *barrios*.

By faith Valerie Bell, although she had lost one

embryo before maturity, determined to trust God to bring her through a full-term pregnancy and to reward her faith with a healthy child. (God did just that. Justin Stephen Bell arrived on February 26, 1979, weighing in at nine pounds and three ounces.)

By faith Lane and Ebeth Dennis adopted a second child of another race to add to their own family of three children when Ebeth knew she was pregnant with another child, because they believed God wanted them to take the unwanted little mulatto into their home.

Many are the saints of God who are living out an active faith. Look around you and add to this list names from your own personal knowledge. Have you trusted God personally and seen him bring your faith to its full bloom? Do members of your immediate family act on their faith? What do you believe God wants you to trust him to do in your life?

The New Scofield Reference Bible tells us, "The essence of faith consists in believing and receiving what God has revealed, and may be defined as that trust in the God of the Scriptures and in Jesus Christ his Son whom he has sent, which receives him as Lord and Savior and impels to loving obedience and good works." Faith is the "confidence that we have in him, that, if we ask any thing according to his will, he heareth us" (1 John 5:14, 15).

In all fairness, we must recognize that not all heroes of the faith lived to see their faith culminate in physical triumph in this world. Many have been tortured or put to death. Some have endured the "trial of cruel mockings and scourgings, yea, moreover, of bonds and imprisonment; they were stoned, they were sawn asunder, were tested, were slain with the sword; they wandered about in sheepskins and goatskins; being destitute, afflicted, tormented'' (Hebrews 11:36, 37). Some died martyrs' deaths, knowing that even though they suffered death at the hands of their tormentors or through burnings at the stake (for example, Tyndale or Savanarola) or being torn from limb to limb by the great snagged teeth of lions, their faith, shining and radiant, would be rewarded by a faithful God, the Righteous Judge.

James 1:22, 23 tells us, ''But be ye doers of the word and not hearers only, deceiving your own selves. For if any be a hearer of the word, and not a doer, he is like a man beholding his natural face in a mirror.'' James later adds, in 2:20, ''Faith without works is dead.'' And in 4:17, ''Therefore, to him that knoweth to do good, and doeth it not, to him it is sin.'' And, ''Behold, we count them happy who endure. Ye have heard of the patience of Job, and have seen the end of the Lord, that the Lord is very pitiful and of tender mercy'' (5:11). ''Elijah was a man subject to like passions as we are, and he prayed earnestly that it might not rain; and it rained not on the earth by the space of three years and six months. And he prayed again, and the heaven gave rain, and the earth brought forth her fruit'' (5:17).

What a comfort it is to realize Elijah was subject to the same passions we are. After the great miracles God had performed for him, he ran away and hid in a cave rather than face the wicked Queen Jezebel. But though his faith had shrunk to the size of a mustard seed, God still honored it and delivered him from his enemies.

In his act of praying, we see Elijah's faith. He didn't say, ''I am nothing. God won't listen to me.'' He allowed the still small voice of God to nourish his faith and to turn his faith from a passive faith hiding in a cave to an active faith confronting a wicked queen.

Are you cowering in a cave? Is there something you feel God would have you do for him? Are you afraid of the Jezebels in your life, afraid to witness for Christ lest you be laughed at and scorned? Have you always wanted to start a Bible study in your home? Bring your faith out of the closet. Polish it and place it on your mantel. Invite your neighbors in for Bible study, believing God will provide a teacher, and he will.

God stands ready to help us when we launch out in faith. He is in the boat with us; we dare not be fearful of doing or daring. We must be ready to hear his voice when he instructs us to cast our nets on the other side, even though we have fished without success all night. Let us pull in our nets in triumph!

Or should they be filled with stingrays and electric eels that threaten our very lives, let us dare even then to pull them in. In our willingness to obey him, even in adversity, he will yet triumph.

"Dare to be a Daniel!" we used to sing boldly in Junior Church. The spirit of that song needs to ring in our hearts in the face of whatever danger, real or imagined, we face. (It is estimated that 90 percent of our anticipated dangers never come to pass. They are products of our fears; faith can free us from these dark dragons.)

Share with the Apostle Paul this high goal: "I have fought a good fight, I have finished my course, I have kept the faith; henceforth there is laid up for me a crown of righteousness, which the Lord, the righteous judge, shall give me at that day; and not to me only, but unto all them also that love his appearing'' (2 Timothy 4:7, 8).

FOOD FOR THOUGHT

1. *List examples from your life where you have put your faith into action.*
2. *List examples from the lives of men and women you know who have put their faith into action.*
3. *List verses you want to memorize on active faith.*

Chapter 10

Fear of Being a Failure or a Pauper

The thing that numbs the heart is this,
That men cannot devise
Some schemes of life to banish fear
That lurks in most men's eyes.

Fear of the lack of shelter, food
And fire for winter's cold,
Fear of their children's lacking these,
This in a world so old.
      —James Norman Hall
      (co-author of *Mutiny on the Bounty*)

When Aleksandr Solzhenitsyn addressed an audience at Harvard soon after coming to America to live, he called this country "the most materialistic nation the world has ever known." His statement received an adverse reaction from both his hearing audience and the press. People do not like to hear the truth when it makes them appear less desirable than they would like.

    Few nations have ever known the luxury and affluence

of our United States—nor the hedonism, the waste of natural resources, the shunning of spiritual values. Rome? Greece? The Aztecs? None has equalled America for productivity. Here every man knows the luxury that once was reserved for kings and potentates. Automobiles? Only the wealthy had horse-drawn chariots. Electricity? The poor were fortunate to own candles, which they generally made themselves. Materially, we are so rich; spiritually, we are so poor.

Materialism is a subtle enemy. John Wesley said, "Money changes people. I never let myself keep it long enough to permit it to affect me." "The love of money is the root of all evil" (1 Timothy 6:10). Men who worship mammon instead of God will do anything to obtain it; money enslaves those who become its worshipers. No matter how much is obtained, it is never enough.

No one living in such a rich, affluent culture as ours can be entirely free from mammon's subtle influence. Consider how much time we spend making new purchases for our home, or shopping in the great stores for luxury items we convince ourselves we "must" have. We give comfort and beauty, the latest styles and fashions a very high priority, no matter what the cost.

We are known as the "throw-away generation." When the toaster doesn't work, out it goes. Instead of saving leftovers for stews and salads, we toss out what we don't eat. Too many of us have forgotten (or never knew) the lessons of the Depression. We no longer remember the jobless, the long soup lines, the penniless times. It is strange but true that even in our society, intrigued with money and what it will buy, many of us suffer from a fear of poverty.

All of my married life, I have kept a good supply of canned food in my kitchen. One of my daughters has said, "Mother's canned goods are her security blanket." Perhaps this is a result of living through the Depression, or perhaps beneath it all is a subtle fear of poverty. We need to remind ourselves of the oft quoted verse:

> Said the robin to the sparrow,
> "I should really like to know
> Why these anxious human beings
> Rush about and worry so."
>
> Said the sparrow to the robin,
> "Friend, I think that it must be
> That they have no Heavenly Father
> Such as cares for you and me."

The Lord used the lilies growing in the field as an example of divine provision without human anxiety.

> "Consider the lilies of the field, how they grow; they toil not, neither do they spin, and yet I say unto you that even Solomon, in all his glory, was not arrayed like one of these. Wherefore, if God so clothe the grass of the field, which today is, and tomorrow is cast into the oven, shall he not much more clothe you, O ye of little faith? Therefore, be not anxious saying, What shall we eat? or, What shall we drink? or, With what shall we be clothed?" (Matthew 6:28-31)

We have misgivings about our savings. Will they last as long as we live, or are we going to be dependent upon the government for our support? Will Social Security still be in existence when we reach retirement age, or will we face old age without monthly help from the government? These are real concerns to those approaching retirement. The antidote to this fear is:

But my God shall supply all your need according to his riches in Christ Jesus. (Philippians 4:19)

Excessive fear of poverty manifests itself in two ways: in miserliness and saving every penny, or in a defiant, exorbitant spending. The first type is the one who fumbles for the check in the restaurant and never pays his share of the expenses. The second type lives in a spend, spend world and is so dominated by buying things that he does not have time to develop or enjoy cultural and spiritual values.

Some people read the *Wall Street Journal* every morning before they read the Bible, or even in place of it. Money is out of all proportion in their lives. Sometimes they save every penny they can for their old age, only to die an early death brought on because they worried over money matters too much. They repeatedly ask, What is it going to cost me? What is there in it for me? What am I going to get out of it?

The basic difference between a healthy fear of poverty and an unhealthy fear of poverty is that healthy fear causes one to live within his income. It is as simple as that—he does not spend more than he earns. He establishes a savings program. When possible, he transfers checking account funds to interest-paying certificates or government bonds. He starts saving money for his children's education when they are small. He realizes that someday his earning ability will cease and makes plans so that his old age will not be plagued by inability to pay for his own bills. He honors God with a tenth of all his earnings, knowing that in this way he is covenanting with God to provide for his money needs (Malachi 3:10).

When a man's life is built around getting instead of

giving, he faces a serious spiritual problem. We need to realize that all of our material possessions are gifts from the Lord. "The silver is mine, and the gold is mine, saith the Lord of hosts" (Haggai 2:8). When we are truly thankful for all that he has given us to use for him, we are not so apt to covet what our neighbors have, or to try to bring our possessions up to their standards. "Let your manner of life be without covetousness, and be content with such things as ye have; for he hath said, I will never leave thee, nor forsake thee. So that we may boldly say, The Lord is my helper, and I will not fear what man shall do unto me" (Hebrews 13:5, 6).

Janet Taylor Caldwell, who has written many best-selling novels, has said, "There is no happiness in this world. . . . There would be few of us who would be born if we knew what life was like." She has been married four times (two of her marriages ended in divorce) and in a newspaper interview claimed she has only known four happy days in her life. Obviously money and success do not guarantee happiness or contentment.

What does then? David tells us in Psalm 37:16, "A little that a righteous man hath is better than the riches of many wicked." The Apostle Paul adds, "Godliness with contentment is great gain" (1 Timothy 6:6). To know Christ is to lose all fear of poverty, for he has promised to take care of all those who trust in him.

The believer must learn to put all of his possessions on God's altar and seek God's direction in the stewardship of all that God has given him. In order to be good stewards, we need the direction of the Holy Spirit in our money management, as in every area of life. We can pray about each financial demand and seek to give our tithes and offerings where he would direct us.

"No servant can serve two masters; for either he will hate the one, and love the other; or else he will hold to the one, and despise the other. Ye cannot serve God and money." (Luke 16:13)

"Choose you this day whom ye will serve." (Joshua 24:15)

We need fear neither poverty nor failure, if we are children of God through Jesus Christ. "I can do all things through Christ, who strengtheneth me" (Philippians 4:13).

When our son started school, he suffered from an "I can't" complex, evidently from trying to compete with his sister who was three years older. Whenever he was called upon to do something, she would immediately say, "Here, Craigy, I'll do it for you." And do it she did, from tying his shoes to drawing pictures with his crayons to racing his cars.

I was greatly perplexed with his refusal to try to draw a picture or paste something with construction paper. He had an adult-sized fear of failure that completely immobilized him. Finally in desperation one day I asked him, "Why don't you draw with your crayons?" He replied, "I can't. I'm afraid I will make a mistake." "But that is the way we learn—by our mistakes," I told him.

Suddenly his round little face broke into a smile. "You mean mistakes are the way we learn?" There at the age of five the fear of failure left him, and we saw him go through all of his school years as an honor student, being on the president's (not the dean's) list consistently in his college and postgraduate years, all because his fear of failure was conquered.

June Callwood writes, "Courage is a private thing. . . . A man who apologizes to his own son may have waded through crocodiles. . . . Courage in its highest form, moral courage, is what makes a man indestructible. And there is a momentum to it. Each act of courage adds to man's faith in himself, in the purpose and dignity of all life. By each brave act he enlarges his ability to be brave—and eventually the process is irreversible" *(Love, Hate, Fear, Anger and the Other Lively Emotions,* Doubleday).

The kindergartener has to draw on a private supply of courage in order to take his crayons in his chubby hand and draw a picture that his classmates might laugh at and his teacher might think stupid. The high schooler perhaps requires a special brand of bravery to stand for right against peer pressures. The adult—whether parent, teacher, policeman, or whatever—must be courageous in being a firm but loving authority figure. The dying old man, even if a strong believer for many years, needs courage to face imminent death.

In everything we do in life there is an element of risk—the risk of failure, the risk of making mistakes, etc. Only the people who never do anything never make errors. The doer refuses to be held back by his mistakes, but rather learns from them.

Sadly, many persons are the victims of unhealthy thinking and they cannot (or do not) sew, or write, or paint, or take a job, or go out for sports. Why? Because they are in bondage to a fear of failure.

There was once a man who failed at everything he tried. He opened a country store; it went bankrupt. He tried to practice law, but lost one case (and client) after another. He was desperately poor and could not support his family. He tried his hand at politics, only to fail miserably in election after election.

But he persisted and eventually success came to him. In fact, he became President of the United States. His name? Abraham Lincoln. Born in dire poverty, he had no fear of poverty. He was not in bondage to the fear of failure. Through his faith in Christ, he found the courage to keep on trying. This same faith and fear of God led him to liberate thousands of blacks living in slavery. This same reverence for God kept him on his knees in prayer throughout the horrendous years of the Civil War, when he saw thousands of young men killed on the battlefields. In his life, and in ours, faith destroys the fear of failure.

In teaching poetry, I often have students with shining degrees in literature who started out to be poets or writers, but have for all practical purposes given up writing. Why? Because they are intimidated by other more gifted and skilled writers. They are afraid of the rejection slip. Unless they can conquer this fear of failure, they will remain unpublished and unread, no matter how gifted they are. Madeleine L'Engle sent her juvenile book *A Wrinkle in Time* to twenty-eight different publishers before she found a publisher who would accept it. The book became a Newberry Award winner. It takes courage to be a writer—courage to risk criticism, courage to lay your inner thoughts open to public viewing, courage to chance rejection.

Many young couples are now deciding not to have children. Why? They fear their children may not turn out to be good citizens and that as parents they will know failure. It takes courage to rear a family, to risk birth defects (250,000 born every year in the United States), to take on the financial responsibility for some twenty years for each child that is welcomed into the family. (Bankers and economists estimate that each child will cost his parents $100,000 from infancy through college.)

Someone asked Teddy Roosevelt what his greatest pleasure in life was. He replied without hesitating, "My children. I would rather spend an evening with my family than with any of the world's notables." Perhaps that is why he permitted his children to roller-skate through the White House halls! Home and family cannot be surpassed when it comes to affording a man or woman great joy in living. However, it is also true that when children are not brought up in the nurture and admonition of the Lord, having no fear of the Lord in their hearts, tragedy and disappointment result. There is no greater joy than to see one's children walking with the Lord.

There is such a thing as a healthy fear of failure. It prevents many a person from entering into a foolhardy business venture, or purchasing "wildcat" oil stock, or entering into other get-rich-quick schemes. In southern Florida it is estimated that 94 percent of all new businesses fail in the first year and often wipe out the life savings of the person or persons who invested in them. Without doing proper research, many start a Florida business on the basis of the peak winter sales. Then April comes, and their customers go north. A healthy fear of failure and the investigative spirit it inspires are helpful.

Failure is not the end of the line. There is remorse when a student fails his studies (especially when he knows his failure has been caused by a lack of effort).

But a low grade is no excuse to drop out of school. It is rather a challenge to prove that he *can* complete a successful course of study.

Failure in marriage carries with it many complicated feelings—guilt, rejection, a sense of failure, a feeling of unrequited love. God does not intend the Christian to fail in marriage. It is a high calling, a covenant of love. Successful marriage requires hard work on the part of both marriage partners, especially when their personalities are not well suited to each other. There is no better guarantee for success in a marriage than that both partners enter into the relationship with the fear of the Lord in their hearts. The Christian enters into marriage knowing that the vows he has spoken are made before and with God as a third partner in the union. When God is given no consideration in decisions, there can be untold problems. It is a serious thing to break a vow made to God, Ruler of the universe.

We can learn from many of our failures, but marriage seldom (if ever) falls into this category. God never intended the sacred institution of marriage to be a trial and error situation. He wanted it rather to be an opportunity for spiritual growth under his guidance.

Paul J. Meyer, a managerial authority, writes:

There is more to be feared in not making mistakes than in making them. Does this sound paradoxical? It's not. The manager who fears making mistakes too much to risk making them, obviously won't make any. But neither will he learn nor grow. He will stand still, or slide backwards while others about him, with the courage to face up to the inevitable risk that is inherent in initiative, will thrust forward. In short, the status of the individual who plays it too safe will be in greater jeopardy than his more venturesome counterpart.

Rather than fear either failure or poverty, we should live confidently, following God's guidance and trusting him to protect and provide. As Katherine Logan put it:

To have faith where you cannot see; to be willing to work on in the dark; to be conscious of the fact that, so long as you strive for the best, there are better things on the way, this in itself is success.

FOOD FOR THOUGHT

1. *Is it possible for a Christian to know failure? Give an example. How should he respond to this?*
2. *How about poverty? Can this be in God's will?*
3. *What has proved helpful to you in the past when you have had to meet failure?*
4. *What verses are your insurance against failure and poverty (or rather for meeting failure and poverty)?*

Chapter 11
Fear of Living and Loving

'Tis better to have loved and lost
Than never to have loved at all.
        —Alfred, Lord Tennyson,
          "In Memoriam"

In the thirty-sixth year of our marriage, my husband was stricken with a debilitating disease which almost overnight destroyed his brilliant mind. At that time I suffered the most severe spiritual testing I had ever experienced. I suspicioned that I was a female version of Job and that the angels of darkness were taunting God with, "If you afflict that which is nearest and dearest to her, see how she will honor you then."

Seven long difficult weeks in the hospital were followed by four more equally difficult weeks in a rehabilitation center. Confronted with unbelievable medical bills, I was faced with the fact that his recovery was dubious. The future looked ominous. The doctors did not think he would ever be able to return home, and would face months of special care in a nursing home.

Toward the end of his stay in the rehabilitation center, I was called before a board of review. I thought the emphasis would be on my husband, but was surprised when their attention was turned upon me. I was told I should be undergoing psychiatric care!

"You are much too controlled, Mrs. Burton," they told me. "You need to kick and scream." Kick and scream? I had not carried on in such a manner since I was a preschooler and I could not imagine a woman of my maturity being expected to revert to a two-year-old's world.

One staff psychologist said, "You are very angry, Mrs. Burton. You need to vent your anger to someone trained in counseling families of persons going through physical and mental disasters." I was not aware of a feeling of anger. I was disappointed that our retirement, to which we had looked forward, had been plunged suddenly into a traumatic experience. But I was not aware that I was angry at anyone. Should I have been angry at God for letting it happen?

I had been trained in the Scriptures from early childhood. I knew that this trial of my faith could only be faced in the light of God's Word and through the comfort of his Holy Spirit. I realized that my counselors were trained in medicine and psychology, but had little, if any, training in the things of God. I knew that my learning to live with and adjust to these difficult conditions depended upon my trusting in God for strength and wisdom. I knew that despite the heavy financial burden the disease placed upon me, God would not fail me in the hour of my spiritual trauma. I could count on him.

In the months that followed, my internist told me he thought it little less than a miracle that during the weeks of my husband's almost vegetablelike condition, I had not shown any sign of stress such as high blood pressure, ulcers, colitis, stroke, etc. My faith had been put to the test, and God had not failed me. Many fears tried to assail me, but by his Spirit God taught me to overcome all fear and to realize the truth of his promise—"For God hath not given us the spirit of fear, but of power, and of love, and of a sound mind" (2 Timothy 1:7).

Courage is the standing army of the soul which keeps it from conquest, pillage and slavery. (Henry Van Dyke)

It takes courage to live! It takes courage to love! There will come a time when the person loved must slip out of your life, and you find yourself loving a memory. It helps to face such a loss when we realize that none of us have control of our lives. Contrary to the famous poem *"Invictus,"* none of us are "captains of our souls." We cannot say how long we shall live, or even in what state or condition we shall live. Our lives are completely in God's hands.

We like to insulate ourselves from suffering and death. Perhaps that is one reason why couples in this age of easy abortion decide not to have children; they have a fear of living and loving. "What if there should be something wrong with our child? What if he should die at an early age and we would have to face deep grief? What if she should grow up rebellious and disgrace us?"

Likewise, some women who do not marry are afraid of living and loving. "What if I should find married life too difficult? What if I could not endure the bearing of children? What if my husband would cease to love me and demand a divorce?'' These fearful women crawl into their cocoons and remain there, afraid of an unhappy marriage. They content themselves with the arrested chrysalis and fail to grow wings and develop into butterflies.

Men, too, are not free from suffering from a fear of living and loving. One young man I know pulled back into his shell after a broken romance and became a victim of his fear. His relationships with women in the future were shallow, surface relationships. He was afraid of getting hurt again. He was afraid to get his feet wet in the stream of life, preferring to remain an observer on the bank.

The fear of living and loving does not belong in the world of the believer. It should be buried deep below the cross and replaced with the resurrection flowers of joyful living.

Especially sad are the elderly couples who pass their days glued to their TV sets, regretting that no one comes to see them, envying other couples who are happily surrounded with children and grandchildren. The poet Dinah Maria Craik wrote:

Love that asketh love again
Finds the barter nought but pain;
Love that giveth in full store
Aye receives as much, and more,

Such a freely given love does not count the cost, nor worry about being loved in return. It is a higher type of love than *phileo* (brotherly love) or *eros* (the mortal love between a man and a woman). It borders on *agape* love, a love that is pure and is like the love God has for his own. This is God's own love implanted in the heart of the believer after he has committed his life to Christ. It is not a human love, but rather divine.

> Grant me the kind of love
> that does not keep old scores.
>
> Let me be unfettered
>   from old tallies
>   from old whiplashes
>   from old borrowing and not returning.
> Let me forget all these.
> The straw-stuffed scarecrow
> kind of love with coat and hat
> retrieved from old trunks—
> let me know none of these.
>   Let me know every morning-new day
>   kind of love: dew-wet, garden-fresh,
>   growing kind of love
> a not-afraid-of-being-hurt
> or wounded kind of love—
> a love that does not shun toll-roads—
> nor yet mind byroads
>   and never counts the cost.
>   (from *I Need a Miracle Today, Lord,*
>   by Wilma Burton, Moody Press)

Gerald Hawthorne, professor of Greek, says that the word *agape* was not used until Christ died on the cross. It was chosen by first-century Christian leaders to describe God's perfect love for man—a type of "stretching love" to stretch to cover faults in others, to accept them as they are.

Agape love might further be described thus: "Love is the willingness to do everything to help and unwilling-ness to do anything to hinder." Love hides a multitude of sins. In Paul's great love chapter, 1 Corinthians 13, he writes:

Love suffereth long, and is kind; love envieth not; love vaunteth not itself, is not puffed up, doth not behave itself unseemly, seeketh not its own, is not easily provoked, thinketh no evil, rejoiceth not in iniquity, but rejoiceth in the truth; beareth all things, believeth all things, hopeth all things, endureth all things. Love never faileth; but whether there be prophecies, they shall be done away; whether there be tongues, they shall cease; whether there be knowledge, it shall vanish away. . . . And now abideth faith, hope, love, these three; but the greatest of these is love. (vv. 4-8, 13)

In his teaching on the love chapter, Professor Hawthorne tells his classes that the Greek reads, "is not provoked"—the adverb "easily" is missing.

Looking at other translations, we find that this love is:

1. "So patient and so kind." *(Williams)* "It meekly and patiently bears ill treatment from others. It is gentle, benign, pervading and penetrating the whole nature, mellowing all which could have been harsh and austere." *(Wuest)*

2. "This love looks for ways of being constructive." *(Phillips)*

3. "It never boils with jealousy, never envies." *(Williams* and *Amplified)*

4. "It is not conceited, arrogant, or inflated with pride." *(Amplified)*

5. "It is neither anxious to impress, nor does it cherish inflated ideas of its own importance." *(Phillips)*

6. "It is not out for display." *(Berkeley)*

7. "It does not act unbecomingly." *(Wuest* and *Amplified)*

8. "It has good manners." *(Phillips)*

9. "It covers up everything." *(Berkeley)*

10. "It does not insist on its own rights or its own way—for it is not self-seeking." *(Amplified)*

11. "It is not possessive." *(Phillips)*

12. "It is not touchy, or fretful, or resentful." *(Amplified)*

13. "It is not irritated, provoked, exasperated, aroused to anger." *(Wuest)*

14. "It takes no account of the evil done to it." *(Amplified)*

15. "It does not count up past wrongs." *(Riverside,* out of print)

16. "It does not gloat over the wickedness of other people. It is glad with good people when truth prevails." *(Phillips)*

17. "Love knows no end to its trust." *(Phillips)*

18. "It has unquenchable faith." *(Berkeley)*

19. "It is ever ready to believe the best of every person." *(Amplified)*

20. "It bears up under anything and everything that comes. Its hopes are fadeless under all circumstances, and it endures everything without weakening." *(Amplified)*

Love does not hide its light under a bushel, but carries a candle wherever it goes, readily sharing its light with those in darkness.

David Enlow in one of his books refers to the following code as "the million dollar secret for success":

Never say anything to a friend, neighbor, or stranger that you do not first ask yourself, "Am I saying this in love?"

I am sure you have known people who have a zest for living. It is fun to be around such people. They seem to enjoy everything they see, everything they do. Walk on the beach with such a person and you end up finding exotic shells, skiffing the surface with stones, removing your shoes and wading into the tide, laughing at being caught by an unexpected wave, enjoying the sun and the spray, buying hot dogs from the refreshment stand, spreading them thickly with mustard and sweet pickles. You return home in the evening feeling renewed in spirit, soul, and body. There is medicine in laughter. Being with such a life-loving person is better than a visit to the doctor's office or a new perscription for medicine.

If you have been withdrawn, a fear of living inhibiting your every action, deliberately choose to be with those who love to live. Allow yourself to laugh with them, to imitate their wholehearted zeal for everyday living.

It is often said that the greatest secret for success is enthusiasm—enthusiasm about what you are doing, enthusiasm for living. When you go into a store and the clerks disappear into a back room, don't you find yourself going quietly out to find a store where you are met with a cheery, "Good morning. What can we do for you today?" The first store soon goes out of business. The second store grows, adds more help, and has to expand into the shop next door. All because of enthusiasm.

Attitude can make all the difference in whether you are happy or morose. Happiness begins on the inside of the person; it does not depend upon circumstances or the weather. It can be chosen. It can become a habit. Just as morose thinking can lead a person into a pit of depression, so healthy thoughts can keep a person on the highway of happiness, and joy can become a live-in house guest.

Love means different things to different people. To the infant crying his demands in his crib, it means "me—me—me!" Sadly, some adults have either never gotten beyond the crib stage or have reverted to it.

The infant must be taught to love. Slowly he learns to love his mother, through her example of loving him. Soon his love grows to include his father and the children in the family, then his playmates and, as he starts to school, his schoolmates. When he reaches his teens, he tumbles into another kind of love, *eros*, the love of a man for a maid. This love may bring a deep sense of fulfillment, or the trauma of unrequited love.

Unfortunately, many people never know the highest from of love: *agape*—Godlike love for the Creator. Only when we have made a life commitment to Christ can we experience *agape* love. This pure form of love cannot be self-centered; rather, it demands to be shared. It is the Christ-light shining in a dark world. It is not a getting love, but is unique because of its giving qualities.

To experience this type of love is to know the greatest antidote for fear and anxiety the world has ever seen. It is the perfect love to which John refers in saying, "Perfect love casteth out fear. . . . He that feareth is not made perfect in love" (1 John 4:18).

This is the love that enables one to see her dearest lowered into the dark, cold earth and not be overcome by the sight, but rather rejoices in the promise of the resurrection.

Let the chrysalis of love fully develop in you, open its cocoon, and on wings of love dare to try first the bush, then the tree, and at last the open sky. Living can be exciting. If you know Christ, there need be no dull days and evenings.

When through commitment to Christ our lives are flooded with *agape* love, we then are able to love family, friend, stranger, and even our enemies for Christ's sake.

It is the perfect love that knows no fear.

Put the old life, the old sins behind you. Thank God for being such a forgiving God, and dare to love with his *agape* love.

Take Christ to the nursing home in your area. Be a friend to someone who is lonely or rejected. Be a minister of love to the bereaved, the rebellious, the addicted, the neglected. Learn to love by loving, and your fears will vanish like fog before a bright sun.

In the nursing home, do not try to befriend every person in the home. Rather, select one or two very lonely individuals, who have no visitors, no friends or family who come to see them. Make such a person a special friend and be willing to meet the expediency of his or her needs. Remember her birthday and Christmas with special gifts. Take her a rose from your picket fence. Or an ice cream sundae (if she is not a diabetic on a special sugar-free diet). Love her with the *agape* love of Christ.

God is Love!

FOOD FOR THOUGHT

1. *Have you known unrequited love, human love that failed?*
2. *Has your love for someone proved inadequate and let that someone down? Some say, "He who ceases to be a friend never was a friend." Have you stopped being a friend to someone you once loved?*
3. *List and describe the three types of love.*
4. *What can you do to develop* agape *love?*
5. *Is devotional life important in living a life of* agape *love?*
6. *Establish a time for your personal devotions, prayer, and reading God's Word.*

Chapter 12
Fear of Powers of Evil

Greater is he that is in you,
than he that is in the world.
   —1 John 4:4

Don Richardson's two books *(Peace Child, Lords of the
Earth)* tell about the work of missionaries in New Guinea
among cannibalistic, demon-worshiping tribes. Here are
twentieth-century tales of people living under oppressive
superstitions, some even sacrificing their own children to
appease blood-thirsty demon gods. Only the gospel of
Jesus Christ can cause them to give up their heathen
practices.

"But I am not living in dark Africa or pagan New
Guinea," you may be protesting. "Why should I, a
citizen of the United States, discuss demons?"

The demons man has worshiped through the centuries
are still here. Only their names have changed. The gods
of money, power, lust, greed, pleasure, alcohol, drugs,
marijuana, cocaine, heroin still enslave and still cause

fear. The drug addict is as surely the victim of a demonic power as if he were slashing his body in front of a pagan god made of clay or stone. Many a man in our society worships the golden calf of money, sometimes lying awake for hours scheming how he can acquire more and more of the green ogre.

A healthy fear of evil will cause us to flee from it, to the protection of God's salvation. For example, a healthy fear of alcohol, recognizing it for what it really is—the leading cause of drug addiction in our country—can be a good thing. The "demon rum" is more than a fictional character. He is a reality, and his chains are strong. Only Christ can successfully release a person from this demon's grasp. Even then, the body is often subject to a lifetime of struggle with cravings that perhaps never really leave.

Paul recognizes in Ephesians 6:12 that "we wrestle not against flesh and blood, but against principalities, against powers, against the rulers of the darkness of this world, against spiritual wickedness in high places." He admonished us to put on "the whole armor of God, that ye may be able to withstand in the evil day, and having done all, to stand" (vs. 13). Instead of fearing evil powers, we should stand against them.

When we look at the terrible results of spiritual darkness such as drives 900 victims to suicide in Guyana, or to commit mass murder as in the blood baths on the continent of Africa, we see the reality of demons. When we hear of murder committed out of homosexual delusions, with some men committing numerous murders, we again are faced with demonic power.

An ostrichlike head-in-the-sand approach to the subject of demons is unrealistic, although frequent in our modern civilization. A medical doctor would in all probability be laughed at by his peers if he were to diagnose demon possession in one of his patients. But the failure of the medical profession to recognize such cases does not eliminate them in any way. The Bible is the foremost authority on the subject, and its authority does not vanish into nothingness just because present medical science calls it into question.

We read in the Bible that when the archangel Michael disputed with Satan over the body of Moses, he "dared not bring against him a railing accusation, but said, The Lord rebuke thee" (Jude 9). Lucifer or Satan once held a high position in Heaven, but when he fell he did not lose all of his power. He is still very much at work in our present world (see 1 Peter 5:8). Although he sometimes appears as "an angel of light" (2 Corinthians 11:14), he is responsible for much of the spiritual darkness around us. In fact, "the god of this world hath blinded the minds of them who believe not" (2 Corinthians 4:4). However, we can rejoice with John that "greater is he that is in you, than he that is in the world" (1 John 4:4). Therefore, we need not fear.

If a person is committed to Christ, and walking closely with him, no demon can have power over him. "Resist the devil, and he will flee from you" (James 4:7). However, the believer who turns from God and enters into sin is in danger of demonic oppression and even in a sense demon possession.

Whether we face Satan's attacks because of our own sins, or because of Satan's special effort to destroy our trust in God (consider the example of Job), all of us who are Christians are tried by Satan in some way or another. When being challenged by Satan, we should exercise courage and determination, not fear. No matter what the testing, through God we can triumph at the finish line.

Wherefore, seeing we also are compassed about with so great a cloud of witnesses, let us lay aside every weight, and the sin which doth so easily beset us, and let us run with patience the race that is set before us, looking unto Jesus, the author and finisher of our faith, who for the joy that was set before him endured the cross, despising the shame, and is set down at the right hand of the throne of God. (Hebrews 12:1, 2)

We are told in Isaiah 14:12-14 that Lucifer fell from Heaven because of his five "I wills."

I will ascend into heaven,
I will exalt my throne above the stars of God;
I will sit also upon the mount of the congregation,
   in the sides of the north,
I will ascend above the heights of the clouds,
I will be like the Most High.

Lucifer's basic sin was that he wanted to be like God.

Satan's greatest ruse in the life of mortals is to persuade them that he does not exist. Satan is not a comical figure in a red suit, with horns and forked tail. He is an evil deceiver, bent on leading souls to damnation. But the person safe in the salvation of Christ can recognize the Enemy through the enlightenment of the Holy Spirit.

I have heard of people who awaken in the night in terror of demons that may be in their rooms, or worse, attempting to take possession of their bodies. Can God deliver from such fears? God can and does. "Greater is he that is in you, than he that is in the world." God protects his children from the power of Satan in their lives. He does not want us to fear evil forces, but to be secure in the knowledge that in Christ we are safe.

When a young man I know was in college, he worked in a state institution for juvenile delinquents. These boys were from the street gangs of Chicago. When my friend increased his hours from eight on guard duty to eight more for practice teaching, the sixteen hours in such an environment proved a great strain on him both physically and mentally. In the cabin assigned to him was a group of so-called "Satan worshipers." He was not particularly alarmed when they made threats against his life and the lives of his family, nor when they bragged about placing a hex on him and told him he would be dead within a short time.

But something strange started to happen to him. When he tried to pray, he found that he could not, and he seemed to be enveloped in a terrible darkness. Concerned for him, and fearing he might suffer a nervous break- down, his wise young wife influenced him to quit his job. But the bad effects followed him into his private living.

We prayed with him and talked freely with him about his problem. He finally analyzed it as demon oppression. A firmly committed Christian, he never experienced actual demon possession, but he did experience a severe degree of demon oppression that was to last several months. Finally he heard of a godly woman who at one time had worked in an asylum for the insane. She, too, had gone through an experience of demon oppression that had caused her to quit her job, but had received help from a minister who was known to cast out demons. Through this woman's prayers, my young friend found release.

We should be on our guard as we approach (or are in)

the so-called "end times" when the power of Satan will increase. This may be what we are seeing in the headlines and in the evil apparent around us. As Christians, we need to ask the Lord, as the archangel Michael did, to rebuke Satan and his hosts. We need to be mindful too of the example of the disciples that came to the Lord after they were unable to cast the demons from a demon-possessed man and Jesus told them, "This kind goeth not out except by prayer and fasting" (Matthew 17:21). *The Lord* has authority against demons, not us.

A healthy fear of the cults can be a good thing too. It can cause us to examine not only the obvious cults which are growing rapidly in our country (Krishna, Zen, Moonism, etc.). We also need to examine more subtle cults that hide behind the mask of liberation and contemporary thinking.

Tom Howard in an article in *Christianity Today* (January 5, 1979) listed several new cults: the self cult, the cult of frankness, the cult of liberation, the cult of the unstructured, the cult of the new morality. We might add to his list the following: the health fad cult, the diet cult, the exercise cult, the sports cult, the credit card cult, the everything-must-be-new cult, the buy-buy cult, etc. Let's examine some of these.

The *self cult* or *me cult* fits the description sociologists have given the seventies—the "me generation." Scripture encourages us to seek God first, trusting him to supply our every need. A healthy fear of this cult will foster unselfish living and full dependence on God.

The *cult of frankness* seeks to consume us. "Be honest. Tell it like it is. If you think it, say it. Don't hold anything back. Communicate." The Christian has a

God-given right to the privacy of his inner thoughts, and does not need to be intimidated by this modern shrine of soul nakedness. The T-groups so popular in behavioral psychology, demanding that every thought be put on the table, is apt to do harm to the psyche. There is "one mediator between God and man" to whom we are responsible to confess our inner thoughts. We do not need to open our very souls to men's sight.

The *cult of liberation* cries, "I am the captain of my soul!" It throws out all of the old mores and taboos. This cult would lead us to believe we have "missed the boat" entirely and now must fashion a better life for our generation. But when we "liberate" ourselves from God's standards and forgiveness, we become slaves to ourselves.

The *cult of the unstructured* is another modern invention that would lead us to believe all structure—whether in music, love sonnets, weddings, or whatever—is passé. But foundations were first created by God when he structured the universe. There must be plan and procedure in every building, every organization. Without it, there would be chaos. The Christian recognizes the importance of the laws of God.

Are you about to be taken in by the *cult of the convenient?* Have you been unduly influenced by its propaganda for abortion and free sex? Biblical ethics and Christian standards of living are necessary to the Great Dance of life. Without the pattern, we stumble over our own feet and fall, often bringing down with us those we love.

The *cult of the new morality* (or as some have rightly called it, the old immorality) has especially found adherents among the ranks of teenagers. In Palm Beach County, Florida last year over 3,000 teenage girls gave birth to babies. Children are bearing children! Conventional morality based on biblical teaching is a protection for both the individual and society. When we are blindly influenced by this cult, we open ourselves to serious guilt complexes, unwanted pregnancies, venereal disease, mental illness, physical and spiritual poverty.

Another cult which is trying to brainwash us is the *everything-new cult,* which causes its adherents to buy all the lastest gadgets on the market—the latest in carpeting, a new refrigerator with the latest in icemakers, a new tabletop stove, the newest stereo, TV, radio. Or there is the *latest-model-car cult,* which insists its members buy the latest model car each year—whether they can afford it or not. These go along with the *credit card cult,* whose victims often find themselves heavily in debt and headed for bankruptcy. These slavery cults keep their followers chained to monthly payments at high interest rates. They lead to poverty and bankruptcy.

Among the more subtle cults is the *divorce cult.* It has gained for its members not only thousands from outside the church, but from inside the church as well.

A young pastor in his first pastorate came to see me one noon upset over a counseling session he had had with a young couple in his church. Hearing they were considering divorce, he phoned them and asked that they come to his study. During the counseling session, the wife revealed that she was on her way to her lawyer's office to file divorce papers. She admitted she had no biblical ground for divorce, but said she had married too young and wanted her freedom. She was tired of sitting home evenings waiting for Mark to come home from work. She was tired of caring for their two-year-old. Mark could keep the little boy. She wanted to have a good time—to be able to date again.

The young minister became impatient with her immaturity. He said, ''Where do you think your course of action is leading you? You are turning your back not only on Mark and your son, but on God and his teachings. If you continue in the direction you are going, you will ruin your life.'' The young wife was shocked—and angry.

Had he been too frank in his advice? The situation was critical and demanded sharp words. His advice was a bitter pill to take, but it proved effective medicine. The wife did not file divorce papers, and after some weeks of separation returned to her husband and child. For the present at least, their marriage has been saved. A weaker pastor might have given them namby-pamby advice and one more child might have suffered a divorced home. But because this pastor chose confident confrontation rather than fear, a family remained together.

How unfortunate, or should I say disastrous, it is for people to try to live without a knowledge of the Word of God. Without it, they are prey to the Satanic cults around them. No years of higher education can protect them from the brainwashings of Scientology or the Unification Church.

There is but one way to be safe and protected from the powers of evil—full faith in Jesus Christ. ''If we walk in the light, as he is in the light, we have fellowship one with another, and the blood of Jesus Christ, his Son, cleanseth us from all sin'' (1 John 1:7). Close fellowship with our Lord can keep us safe from demons, strange cults, and all other evil powers.

FOOD FOR THOUGHT
1. List as many new cults as you can discern.

2. Which of these do you find yourself sometimes following?
3. What is the best protection against evil powers?
4. List verses from God's Word that protect you against
   evil. Memorize them.

Chapter 13
Fear of Death and Dying

And so beside the Silent Sea
I wait the muffled oar.
I know not where His islands lift
their fronded palms in air,
I only know I cannot drift
Beyond His love and care.
        —John Greenleaf Whittier,
          "The Eternal Goodness"

A child does not need to be very old before he develops a fear of death. His dog is struck by a car, and the wagging of the tail ceases. Death has claimed the faithful pet. The child weeps in grief. A new fear is born—the fear of death. "Am I going to die?" he asks his parents. The parent perhaps replies, "Yes, you might if you run into the street," trying to stress safety.

Later when someone in his family or a friend's family sickens and dies, the child learns that there is also another cause of death—disease. "Am I going to get sick and die?'' he asks. A brush-off answer may leave the child with an unwholesome fear of death that may plague him for years. The wise parent will explain that everything living will some day die; but for those who love Jesus, God's Son, death is only a passing from this world into Heaven. Many a person has a hypochondriacal fear of illness and death because some adult did not take the time to explain death and dying when he first became aware of it.

One small boy who lost his mother at the age of five held an anger in his heart for many years because someone told him as he stood weeping beside his mother's casket, ''God took her.'' He hated God for taking his beloved mother away. No doubt the adult who spoke those words had no idea of the effect they would have on the small boy's life.

My grandmother died when I was four and I was lifted up by an aunt to see her sleeping in her casket. ''She has gone to Heaven,'' was the explanation. Soon after I started to school, the mother of a boy in my class died. I developed a fear of death and was afraid my own mother might die. This took the form of an obsession that I carried needlessly through all my childhood; my mother lived to be eighty-eight. No one knew I harbored such a fear, but I would awaken in the night and lie trembling in my bed. When morning came, I would rush into my mother's room to be sure she was still alive.

Death is no stranger to me. Several times I have hung over its precipice, not knowing whether or not I would slip over the brink. At the age of twenty-four, I was critically ill from endocarditis, a serious inflammation of the heart valves as a result of rheumatic fever. Before the days of penicillin, the prognosis was that only one out of a hundred lived, and that survivor would be an invalid for the rest of his life. My pastor, a God-fearing man (who later became chaplain to the leprosarium in Carville, Louisiana) sat by my bed daily and literally prayed me from death to life—and health. Four months after the attack, when I returned to the doctor's office he exclaimed, "You are a walking miracle!" A miracle of God's healing power and grace.

The doctors who attended me, however, were somewhat skeptical and advised me never to marry, nor to risk having children. This advice I ignored and when God led the "right man" into my life, we married and had three extremely healthy children. Another miracle of faith over fear!

Up to a certain point, the fear of death can be a healthy thing. It contributes to the preservation of life. It is good for the child to realize the dangers that lurk in the streets, or to know that eating good food brings good health. But when he is afraid that any illness his mother has will result in death, his fear has become morbid and harmful.

When I was new to air travel, I had an experience that made me realize how much the believer's faith helps maintain peace in her soul. My plane was late in taking off from the Salt Lake City airport. After an hour delay, an air force colonel and an army officer from Germany sat on either side of me. Both men were highly agitated by the bad flying conditions. They discussed the possibility of leaving the plane and hiring an automobile to drive through the snowy mountains, but decided against the idea. As we took off into the falling snow, I could see the two men were full of fear.

As we approached a landing in Butte, one asked me, "How can you stay so calm through all of this?" I dared not tell them it was only my second air flight, or they would have thought me too stupid to recognize the danger involved in flying in a storm in the mountains. I had heard of downdrafts. I could see the mountaintops that loomed suddenly out of the clouds on first the left and then the right. But I knew no fear. I told them, "If this plane goes down, I know I shall be instantly with the Lord in Heaven. That is why I am not afraid."

I was not born a lion of courage. In my early years, I was often a trembling kitten with my back arched and my fur standing straight on my back. *But God. . .*, as Dr. V. Raymond Edman titled his book, has made all the difference. In the face of situations that completely fill the unbeliever with fear, I have known the "peace of God, which passeth all understanding" (Philippians 4:7). The calm I knew on the plane baffled my veteran flight companions. Since then I have flown hundreds of times, and often through turbulent weather. While I have no love for sudden air pockets, God has always given the peace that has kept me from having a fear of death. He gives us the grace to meet any of life's situations—not before—but at the time we must meet them. Like the manna the children of Israel gathered daily in the wilderness, the grace to meet life's difficult situations is not given ahead of time. Like the manna, it must be received from God as we need it.

When we realize that our lives are in God's hands, and that he will take us home in his time, a giant step has been taken toward overcoming the fear of death. Also helpful is living with all of our business affairs in order, keeping relationships with people pleasing to God and being committed to him, living each day according to what we understand to be his will for us. Do all this and we will have no fear of death.

God is our shield from any and all danger. Only what he permits—through his infinite love—can touch his child. Only what he deems best for spiritual development can possibly reach his beloved.

It is easier to be free from a fear of death for one's self than for our loved ones. When a child sets out on a long and perilous journey, a parent can know many fears for that child's safety. Here again it is a matter of commitment. Commit that child to God's perfect love and be free from fear. "But first I must warn that child of this danger and that danger . . ." All right, but use just as many words to assure him or her of God's power to protect and keep safely.

Yea, though I walk through the valley of the shadow of death, I will fear no evil; for thou art with me; thy rod and thy staff they comfort me. Thou preparest a table before me in the presence of mine enemies; thou anointest my head with oil; my cup runneth over. Surely goodness and mercy shall follow me all the days of my life; and I will dwell in the house of the Lord forever. (Psalm 23:4-6)

The 23rd Psalm is a beautiful antidote to the fear of death. David wrote then in the face of daily threats to his life by the bear, the lion, the cougar as he guarded his sheep. But we can repeat these words now in the face of the daily threat of dangers we must face, be it airplane crash, automobile accident, positive tests for cancer, high blood pressure, emphysema, heart disease, etc.

I was teaching my small daughter the story of the

disciples with Jesus in their boat, and the fact that they were not afraid. She spoke up excitedly, "Oh, I wouldn't be afraid with Jesus in my boat either, would you?" No, I emphatically would not—but I have to admit, there have been times I failed to recognize his presence in the boat with me. Practicing the presence of God dispels fear.

Jesus is in your boat! When the death waves threaten to capsize you, call upon him and he will not fail to calm the waters outside, as well as the hidden waves that may be surging within. "Lo, I am with you always," Jesus promised (Matthew 28:20).

Last week I found myself driving into the city of Miami on what has been called the heaviest trafficked expressway in the world, I-95. My praying went something like this: "Dear Lord, how is it that I, a simple country girl, should ever end up driving in such heavy city traffic alone?" A voice answered me clearly, "But you are not alone!" Indeed, I wasn't. The Christian believer is never alone. His or her closest Friend is always by his or her side.

Practice the presence of God in the lonely airport in the wee morning hours, whenever you must drive alone on strange routes, when you must stay overnight in strange motels or in strange cities or in a hospital. If you are a Christian, you are never alone, not even when the time comes for Christ to call you home, through the dark corridor and into his waiting Presence. He, your Lord and Savior, will receive you with a warm welcome, more warm than any you have known in this life.

We picture death as coming to destroy; let us rather picture Christ as coming to save. We think of death as ending; let us rather think of life as beginning, and that more abundantly. We think of losing; let us think of gaining. We think of parting; let us think of meeting. We think of going away; let us think of arriving. And as the voice of death whispers, "You must go from earth," let us hear the voice of Christ saying, "You are but coming to me!" (Norman Macleod)

Paul cried defiantly in 1 Corinthians 15:54, 55, "Death is swallowed up in victory. O death, where is thy sting? O grave, where is thy victory?" Therefore, "Ye have not received the spirit of bondage again to fear; but ye have received the Spirit of adoption, whereby we cry, Abba, Father" (Romans 8:15). This is a message of unequalled joy.

You might ask, "How can I be joyful when I have lost my child, or my husband, or my wife?" Or, "How is it possible to know joy when I have an incurable disease and only death is ahead of me?"

The Gestalt approach asks each person to own his own feelings and take responsibility for them. We are not allowed to cop out with "She makes me unhappy," "She makes me angry," "He causes me pain." Each is responsible for his or her own pain, unhappiness, joy. We have the power now, in Christ, to become whatever we want to be, to feel as much love or anger or joy as we want to feel. Lincoln said, "A man can be as happy as he chooses to be."

Move on from the statement "worm that I am," to the truth of the gospel that says, "I am made in the image of God, God loves me."

What shall separate us from the love of Christ? Shall tribulation, or distress, or persecution, or famine, or nakedness, or peril, or sword? . . . I am persuaded that neither death, nor life, nor angels, nor principalities, nor powers, nor things present, nor things to come, nor height, nor depth, nor any other creation shall be able to separate us from the love of God. which is in Christ Jesus, our Lord. (Romans 8:35, 38, 39)

Death is only to be feared if it precedes judgment, and the Christian need not fear any coming judgment. God is both our Judge and Savior.

Who shall lay any thing to the charge of God's elect? Shall God that justifieth? Who is he that condemneth? Shall Christ that died, yea rather, that is risen again, who is even at the right hand of God, who also maketh intercession for us? (Romans 8:33, 34)

The Judge, the Righteous Judge, is interceding for us! The possessor of eternal life need have no fear of death or dying.

The "higher critics" of the Bible have tried to make it appear that Jesus deliberately carried out specific prophecies to make people think he was the Christ. There are some 300 prophecies that were foretold by various prophets in the Old Testament and then actually carried out in the New Testament. It would be an impossibility for one man to fulfill the detailed incidents contained in these prophecies—unless that man were God! We examine a few of these prophecies as a ground for the faith of the believer:

Born in David's lineage	Isaiah 11:1; Luke 1:32
Born of a virgin	Isaiah 7:14; Matt. 1:22, 23
Born at Bethlehem	Micah 5:2; Matt. 2:4-6
Massacre of children	Jer. 31:15; Matt. 2:16-18
Escape to Egypt	Hosea 11:1; Matt. 2:15
Anointed by Spirit	Isaiah 61:1, 2; Luke 4:17-21
Entry to Jerusalem on an ass	Zech. 9:9; Matt. 21:4, 5
Betrayal by friend	Psalm 41:9; John 13:18

Forsaken by disciples	Zech. 13:6; Matt. 26:31
Sold for thirty pieces of silver	Zech. 11:12, 13;
potter's field	Matt. 26:15; 27:3-10
The spitting and buffeting	Isaiah 50:6; Matt. 27:30
Vinegar and gall	Psalm 69:21; Matt. 27:34, 48
No bones broken	Exodus 12:46; John 19:33
Feet and hands pierced	Psalm 22:16; John 20:25
Garments divided by lot	Psalm 22:18; John 19:23, 24
Malefactors and rich men	Isaiah 53:9; Matt. 27:38, 57-60

A study of the fulfilled prophecies are a great inducement to faith in the believer, and can cause the unbeliever to come to a saving knowledge of Christ. If we trust in him, we don't need to fear anything we face, including death.

The fear of death and dying was the last fear to be conquered by our Lord (see Hebrews 2:14, 15). It is also the last fear to be overcome by the believer. Through a study of the Word of God, by applying its truths to our lives, we can learn to overcome not only the fear of dying, but all of the other fears that plague us.

The emotions, the intellect, and the will must all be yielded to Christ in order to possess the kind of faith. hope, and love that casts out the fear of death and enables us to live a life free from unhealthy fear.

"God has not given us the spirit of fear, but of power. and of love, and of a sound mind" (2 Timothy 1:7).

FOOD FOR THOUGHT

1. Do you suffer from a fear of dying?
2. For yourself? For someone you love?
3. Has a fear of dying ever been a problem in the past? Why?

4. *If so, how did you overcome such a fear?*
5. *If you were unable to overcome such a fear in the past, can you now?*
6. *God says, "My grace is sufficient for you." Does he give dying grace before we need it? Can we be certain he will give it to us in abundance when it is needed?*
7. *List and memorize verses on grace and dying, including the 23rd Psalm.*

Afterword

When my husband went to be with the Lord, death came peacefully. God simply took him home. "Mark the perfect man, and behold the upright; for the end of that man is peace" (Psalm 37:37). His perfection was not his own; rather, he stood before God in the perfection of Christ, clothed in his righteousness (see Psalm 132:9; Philippians 3:9), which he had received forty years before.

We had known for several days that he was going to die. There had been a lessening of his vital signs. His respiration dropped to six a minute compared to the normal twenty, and his pulse grew weaker and hard to find. The nurses moved a bed into his room, so I could be with him around the clock; I wanted to be with him in his dying. Our children formed an hour by hour vigil. Valerie, who had inherited his gift of music, sang hymn after hymn, so that he literally went to Heaven on the wings of a song. We held his hands and spoke words of encouragement as we saw him slipping from us.

I told him, "God is going to take you home. Are you trusting in the Lord Jesus?" His head nodded, and a barely audible "yes" came from his lips in reply.

One of the nurses commented she had never known a family to stay with a dying member. She had seen people afraid of the death scene and panic in the eyes of the dying. "However," she commented, "he is going very peacefully and there seems to be no fear whatever in this room."

There was indeed no fear. It was displaced by a realization of the presence of the Lord; he sustained us and supported us through the trying hours. After the long night's vigil, death came at 6:10 in the morning. He slept in the arms of his Maker. There were tears in the eyes of the nurses who had cared for him for many months, and who loved him; my daughter Karen and I were dry-eyed.

"This is no time for tears, mother," she said. "We should be shouting 'hallelujah!' He is entering Heaven! What a glorious moment for him!"

I heard one comment over and over in the days that followed, at the visitation, at the funeral and afterwards—"He was the best friend I ever had." My heart echoed the remark. He had a capacity, as few persons do, for long and lasting friendships.

We knew the peace that passes all understanding at his bedside, during the funeral and burial, and in the days of healing that followed his dying.

On returning from Washington, D.C., where the magazine I edit has its headquarters, I found a notice in my mailbox that the marker had been set at the grave. I knew I should go to the cemetery and check it out before I paid the balance due, but for some reason I found myself dreading the visit. I wondered if I would be devastated at seeing the name I loved so long enscribed in bronze. Would I suffer a deep depression that would be difficult to overcome? I was grateful when my mother, who was then eighty-seven, volunteered to go with me.

Strangely, as I walked across the grass toward the memorial, the quivering in my legs left. A feeling of strength surged through me. As my eyes fell on the bronze marker gleaming golden in the sun, all grief suddenly vanished and I was filled with joy—resurrection joy! It was an ecstasy I do not remember experiencing before.

I had harbored a little regret that I had not changed our grave lots from the extreme east of Chapel Hill Gardens to a more scenic spot near the lake. That regret, too, left me. Suddenly I realized we had ringside seats on Jerusalem! I was filled with the truth of the resurrection. I knew that on resurrection day I would be reunited with my husband and that together in our bodies we would see our Creator. My mind filled with the "Hallelujah Chorus" in a strange and supernatural way.

"I am the resurrection, and the life" (John 11:25). The truth of Jesus' words flooded my being. He did not say, "There is going to be a resurrection" or "I shall cause the resurrection to take place." Rather, *"I am the resurrection!"*

No truer words have ever been spoken. I knew then and know now that I can trust him who has said, "I am the way, the truth, and the life; no man cometh unto the Father, but by me" (John 14:6).

I knew that strange contentment Paul must have known in prison: "I have learned, in whatever state I am, in this to be content'' (Philippians 4:11). I wear no widow's weeds, no black clothing. Instead, I am clothed in Christ's righteousness and stand without fear in his resurrection promise.

Abraham Lincoln said, ''A man can be as happy as he chooses to be.'' Sorrow had rutted his face—the debilitating grief he knew over the death of Anne Rutledge, the deeper tragedy of the Civil War. But he was known for his wit and humor. He had learned that pain and joy can live together and when they do, in the Christian, joy triumphs! Fear must go underground, and faith is free to climb the hills in joy.

FAITH IS A QUIET THING

It does not come shouting
down the hill
nor roaring from the stream—
    It is a slender crocus stem
    pushing through the glacier ice
    a seedling breaking
    through the frozen clod.
It is not a restless wind
seething on the plain—
it rather owns the stillness
of a gentle autumn rain.
    Faith is a quiet thing—
    it mustard seeds its way
    and where it goes
    the heart can hum, can sing!
Faith is not a lion
with a golden mane—
Faith is a newborn lamb
free of spot, of stain.

                                    Wilma Burton

LIVING WITHOUT FEAR CALENDAR

January

1 Gen. 15:1
2 Gen. 21:17
3 Gen. 26:24
4 Gen. 35:17
5 Gen. 43:23
6 Gen. 46:3
7 Gen. 50:19
8 Gen. 50:21
9 Ex. 14:13
10 Ex. 20:20
11 Num. 14:9
12 Num. 21:34
13 Deut. 1:21
14 Deut. 3:2
15 Deut. 3:22
16 Deut. 20:3
17 Deut. 31:6
18 Josh. 10:8
19 Josh. 10:25
20 Deut. 31:8
21 Josh. 8:1
22 1 Chron. 28:20
23 Judg. 6:10
24 Judg. 6:23
25 Ruth 3:11
26 1 Sam. 4:20
27 1 Sam. 12:20
28 1 Sam. 22:23
29 1 Sam. 23:17
30 2 Sam. 9:7
31 1 Kings 17:13

February

1 Prov. 3:25
2 2 Kings 6:16
3 2 Kings 17:34
4 1 Chron. 16:30
5 2 Chron. 20:17
6 Neh. 7:2
7 Job 15:4
8 Job 39:22
9 Psa. 55:19
10 Psa. 5:7
11 Isa. 35:4
12 Isa. 41:10
13 Isa. 43:5
14 Isa. 41:13
15 Isa. 41:14
16 Isa. 43:1
17 Isa. 44:2
18 Jer. 30:10
19 Jer. 46:27
20 Jer. 46:28
21 Isa. 44:8
22 Isa. 51:7
23 Isa. 54:4
24 Jer. 5:22
25 Lam. 3:57
26 Ezek. 3:9
27 Dan. 10:12
28 Dan. 10:19

March		*April*	
1	Joel 2:21	1	1 Chron. 16:30
2	Zeph. 3:16	2	Heb. 12:28
3	Hag. 2:5	3	Neh. 7:2
4	Zech. 8:13	4	Job 1:9
5	Zech. 8:15	5	Job 11:15
6	Mal. 3:5	6	Psa. 27:1
7	Matt. 1:20	7	Psa. 27:3
8	Matt. 10:26	8	Psa. 31:19
9	Matt. 10:28	9	Psa. 34:9
10	Matt. 10:31	10	Psa. 56:4
11	Luke 12:7	11	Psa. 118:6
12	Matt. 28:5	12	Psa. 66:16
13	Luke 1:13	13	Psa. 76:7
14	Luke 1:30	14	Psa. 86:11
15	Luke 2:10	15	Psa. 115:11
16	Luke 5:10	16	Psa. 119:74
17	Luke 8:50	17	Prov. 3:7
18	Luke 12:32	18	Prov. 10:27
19	Luke 21:26	19	Prov. 24:21
20	John 12:15	20	Prov. 31:30
21	Acts 27:24	21	Eccl. 3:14
22	Rev. 1:17	22	Eccl. 5:7
23	Heb. 10:27	23	Eccl. 12:13
24	Heb. 10:31	24	Isa. 8:12
25	Rev. 21:8	25	Isa. 35:4
26	Psa. 139:14	26	Isa. 41:10
27	Psa. 55:5	27	Isa. 43:1
28	Isa. 21:4	28	Isa. 43:5
29	Isa. 33:14	29	Isa. 44:2
30	Josh. 22:25	30	Jer. 5:24
31	Mark 5:33		

May

1 Jer. 10:7
2 Jer. 33:9
3 Dan. 6:26
4 Zeph. 3:7
5 Jer. 1:8
6 Gen. 20:11
7 2 Sam. 23:3
8 2 Chron. 20:29
9 Neh. 5:9
10 Neh. 5:15
11 Psa. 36:1
12 Rom. 3:18
13 2 Chron. 17:10
14 2 Chron. 14:14
15 2 Cor. 7:1
16 2 Chron. 19:7
17 2 Chron. 19:9
18 Job 28:28
19 Psa. 19:9
20 Psa. 34:11
21 Psa. 111:10
22 Prov. 1:7
23 Prov. 9:10
24 Prov. 1:29
25 Prov. 2:5
26 Prov. 8:13
27 Prov. 10:27
28 Prov. 14:26
29 Prov. 14:27
30 Prov. 15:16
31 Prov. 15:33

June

1 Prov. 23:17
2 Isa. 2:10
3 Isa. 2:19
4 Isa. 2:21
5 Isa. 11:2
6 Isa. 11:3
7 Isa. 33:6
8 Acts 9:31
9 Psa. 2:11
10 Matt. 28:8
11 Luke 5:26
12 Luke 8:37
13 2 Cor. 7:15
14 Eph. 6:5
15 Phil. 2:12
16 Heb. 11:7
17 1 Pet. 2:18
18 1 Pet. 3:2
19 Jude 23
20 Psa. 56:4
21 Psa. 66:16
22 Luke 1:74
23 1 Cor. 16:10
24 Phil. 1:14
25 Jude 12
26 Lev. 19:3
27 Num. 14:9
28 Deut. 4:10
29 Deut. 5:29
30 Deut. 28:58

Living Without Fear

July	August
1 Gen. 42:18	1 Isa. 14:3
2 Ex. 15:11	2 Isa. 14:16
3 Ex. 18:21	3 Isa. 25:3
4 1 Kings 8:40	4 Isa. 35:4
5 1 Kings 8:43	5 Isa. 59:19
6 2 Kings 17:38	6 Jer. 10:7
7 2 Kings 17:39	7 Jer. 23:4
8 1 Chron. 16:30	8 Jer. 32:39
9 2 Chron. 6:31	9 Jer. 32:40
10 2 Chron. 6:33	10 Psa. 19:9
11 Job 15:4	11 Dan. 6:26
12 Neh. 1:11	12 Eccl. 5:7
13 Psa. 9:20	13 Eccl. 12:13
14 Psa. 23:4	14 Mic. 7:17
15 Psa. 31:19	15 1 Chron. 16:25
16 Psa. 40:3	16 Ezek. 34:28
17 Psa. 49:5	17 Hag. 1:12
18 Psa. 60:4	18 Mal. 3:16
19 Psa. 61:5	19 Mal. 4:2
20 Psa. 64:9	20 Mark 4:40
21 Psa. 72:5	21 Luke 12:5
22 Psa. 86:11	22 Rom. 8:15
23 Psa. 96:9	23 Rom. 11:20
24 Psa. 102:15	24 Eph. 5:21
25 Psa. 119:39	25 2 Cor. 11:3
26 Psa. 119:63	26 2 Cor. 12:20
27 Psa. 119:74	27 1 Tim. 5:20
28 Psa. 119:79	28 2 Tim. 1:7
29 Psa. 139:14	29 Heb. 4:1
30 Eccl. 3:14	30 Heb. 11:23
31 Isa. 8:13	31 Rev. 14:7

September

1 Lev. 19:32
2 Lev. 25:17
3 Lev. 25:36
4 Lev. 25:43
5 Job 1:9
6 Psa. 66:16
7 Psa. 34:4
8 Eccl. 8:12
9 Eccl. 12:13
10 Isa. 29:23
11 Luke 23:40
12 Acts 13:16
13 1 Pet. 2:17
14 Gen. 32:11
15 Gen. 42:18
16 Deut. 13:4
17 Deut. 13:11
18 Deut. 17:13
19 Deut. 19:20
20 Deut. 21:21
21 2 Kings 17:36
22 Job 37:24
23 Psa. 22:23
24 Psa. 22:25
25 Psa. 25:14
26 Psa. 33:18
27 Psa. 34:7
28 Psa. 34:9
29 Psa. 67:7
30 Deut. 6:2

October

1 Psa. 85:9
2 Psa. 103:11
3 Psa. 103:13
4 Psa. 103:17
5 Luke 1:50
6 Psa. 111:5
7 Psa. 145:19
8 Psa. 147:11
9 Matt. 10:28
10 Luke 12:5
11 Rev. 19:5
12 Psa. 5:7
13 Deut. 6:13
14 Deut. 10:20
15 2 Kings 17:39
16 Deut. 6:24
17 Deut. 10:12
18 Deut. 14:23
19 Deut. 17:19
20 Deut. 31:12
21 Deut. 31:13
22 Josh. 4:24
23 Josh. 24:14
24 Col. 3:22
25 1 Sam. 12:14
26 1 Sam. 12:24
27 2 Kings 4:1
28 2 Kings 17:28
29 Psa. 5:7
30 Psa. 15:4
31 Psa. 22:23

November

1 Psa. 33:8
2 Psa. 34:9
3 Psa. 115:11
4 Psa. 115:13
5 Psa. 118:4
6 Psa. 135:20
7 Prov. 3:7
8 Prov. 24:21
9 Heb. 13:6
10 Jer. 26:19
11 Hos. 3:5
12 Jonah 1:9
13 Ex. 1:17
14 Ex. 1:21
15 Neh. 7:2
16 Job 1:1
17 Acts 10:2
18 Josh. 1:9
19 1 Sam. 12:18
20 1 Kings 18:3
21 Psa 56:3
22 Psa. 89:7
23 Matt. 27:54
24 Ex. 14:31
25 2 Kings 17:32
26 2 Kings 17:33
27 2 Kings 17:41
28 Hos. 10:3
29 Jonah 1:16
30 Mal. 3:16

December

1 Gen. 22:12
2 Isa. 51:12
3 Isa. 57:11
4 Job 1:8
5 Job 2:3
6 Psa. 25:12
7 Psa. 91:5
8 Psa. 112:1
9 Psa. 112:7
10 Psa. 128:1
11 Psa. 128:4
12 Prov. 13:13
13 Prov. 14:2
14 Prov. 14:16
15 Prov. 31:30
16 Eccl. 7:18
17 Eccl. 8:13
18 Isa. 50:10
19 Acts 10:22
20 Acts 10:35
21 Acts 13:26
22 1 John 4:18
23 Ex. 15:11
24 Deut. 20:8
25 Judg. 7:3
26 Deut. 28:58
27 Prov. 29:25
28 Matt. 8:26
29 Mark 4:40
30 Luke 21:11
31 Rev. 15:4

CHRISTIAN HERALD ASSOCIATION AND ITS MINISTRIES

CHRISTIAN HERALD ASSOCIATION, founded in 1878, publishes The Christian Herald Magazine, one of the leading interdenominational religious monthlies in America. Through its wide circulation, it brings inspiring articles and the latest news of religious developments to many families. From the magazine's pages came the initiative for CHRISTIAN HERALD CHILDREN'S HOME and THE BOWERY MISSION, two individually supported not-for-profit corporations.

CHRISTIAN HERALD CHILDREN'S HOME, established in 1894, is the name for a unique and dynamic ministry to disadvantaged children, offering hope and opportunities which would not otherwise be available for reasons of poverty and neglect. The goal is to develop each child's potential and to demonstrate Christian compassion and understanding to children in need.

Mont Lawn is a permanent camp located in Bushkill, Pennsylvania. It is the focal point of a ministry which provides a healthful "vacation with a purpose" to children who without it would be confined to the streets of the city. Up to 1000 children between the ages of 7 and 11 come to Mont Lawn each year.

Christian Herald Children's Home maintains year-round contact with children by means of an *In-City Youth Ministry*. Central to its philosophy is the belief that only through sustained relationships and demonstrated concern can individual lives be truly enriched. Special emphasis is on individual guidance, spiritual and family counseling and tutoring. This follow-up ministry to inner-city children culminates for many in financial assistance toward higher education and career counseling.

THE BOWERY MISSION, located at 227 Bowery, New York City, has since 1879 been reaching out to the lost men on the Bowery, offering them what could be their last chance to rebuild their lives. Every man is fed, clothed and ministered to. Countless numbers have entered the 90-day residential rehabilitation program at the Bowery Mission. A concentrated ministry of counseling, medical care, nutrition therapy, Bible study and Gospel services awakens a man to spiritual renewal within himself.

These ministries are supported solely by the voluntary contributions of individuals and by legacies and bequests. Contributions are tax deductible. Checks should be made out either to CHRISTIAN HERALD CHILDREN'S HOME or to THE BOWERY MISSION.

Administrative Office: 40 Overlook Drive, Chappaqua, New York 10514
Telephone: (914) 769-9000